BRIDGING
THE SILENCE

A NORTON PROFESSIONAL BOOK

BRIDGING THE SILENCE

*Nonverbal Modalities
in the Treatment of Adult Survivors
of Childhood Sexual Abuse*

Susan L. Simonds, M.A., M.C.A.T.

W.W. NORTON & COMPANY, INC. • *NEW YORK* • *LONDON*

Composition by Bytheway Typesetting Services, Inc.
Manufacturing by Haddon Craftsmen, Inc.

Library of Congress Cataloging-in-Publication Data
Simonds, Susan L.
    Bridging the silence : nonverbal modalities in the treatment of
adult survivors of childhood sexual abuse / Susan L. Simonds.
        p. cm.
    "A Norton professional book"—P. preceding t.p.
    Includes bibliographical references and index.
    ISBN 0-393-70175-1
    1. Adult child sexual abuse victims—Rehabilitation.   2. Nonverbal
communication (Psychology)   I. Title.
    [DNLM: 1. Child Abuse, Sexual—therapy.   2. Psychotherapy-
-methods.   3. Movement.   4. Psychotherapy—in adulthood.   WM
450.5.A8 S597b   1994]
RC569.5.A28S56   1994
616.85'83690651—dc20
DNLM/DLC   93-46998   CIP
for Library of Congress

W. W. Norton & Company, Inc., 500 Fifth Avenue, New York, NY 10110
W. W. Norton & Company, Ltd., 10 Coptic Street, London WC1A 1PU

2   3   4   5   6   7   8   9   0

To Roz
whose friendship strengthened my voice.

CONTENTS

LIST OF FIGURES

ACKNOWLEDGMENTS

I WANT TO THANK the many clients and patients who have worked with me through the years, allowing me to share in their struggles and creativity. I want to particularly extend my appreciation to W. J., R. S., M. D., and F. B. for allowing their artwork to be used in this book.

My dear friend, Roz Brumfield, who has extensive experience with creative therapies, has been incredibly patient in listening to my every anxiety and excitement, while offering support, wisdom, and humor. I am especially grateful to David Perry and Bernice Schneyer for their suggestions, encouragement, and thorough readings of the manuscript. Tina Krovetz has not only given her constant emotional support, but also lent her expertise with photographing the artwork; her pastel on the book jacket has been in my office for many years. I am appreciative of the colleagues, friends, and family who generously gave me feedback, resources, information, and various forms of help: Mary DeArment, Kathy Diak, Sherry Goodall, Alison Hall, Ron Hays, Luisa Horn, Mindy Jacobson, Carol Just, Cathy McCoubrey, Kathy Miller, Trish Miron, Roslyn Rivkin, Joan Roddy, John Sappington, David Simonds, Nina Simonds, Henry Sommer, Liz Templeton, and Mary Ann Venezia.

I want to acknowledge the important roles that Dianne Dulicai and Myra Levick played in my development as a therapist.

My editor, Susan Barrows Munro, who had enthusiasm for this project from its inception, has been wonderful.

INTRODUCTION

DURING THE LAST 15 years, I have worked as a clinician, trainer, program developer, and administrator in inpatient, outpatient, and partial hospital settings. I have worked as a movement therapist, creative arts therapist, psychotherapist, and group therapist. I have had the opportunity to develop a mental health center for women, to create an inpatient treatment program for sexually abused women, and to establish outpatient services for women. About five years ago, I saw a change in my referrals. Colleagues were referring many more individuals for art and movement therapies with explanations such as, the client "can't talk about anything" or "needs help in being more expressive." As it turned out, all of these clients were women who had a history of childhood sexual abuse. At the same time, I began to see many more identified survivors of sexual abuse who were looking for a therapist with training in creative arts therapy.

In my experience, adult survivors of childhood sexual abuse have a special affinity for nonverbal modalities, i.e., visual imagery, kinesthetic imagery, and body movement. These modalities are basic elements of art psychotherapy and movement psychotherapy.

My goal in writing this book is to integrate nonverbal modalities into verbal psychotherapy with adult survivors. For the nonspecialist therapist with little or no training in using art or movement in psychotherapy, this book offers safe, detailed suggestions for using nonverbal modalities. For the specialist therapist, this book places nonverbal interventions within the context of goal-specific treatment phases for adult survivors. My hope is to make nonverbal treatment interventions accessible to nonspecialist therapists while offering specialist therapists an expanded framework within which to apply their skills.

The clients described in this book are prototypes of real clients; the identifying characteristics and events have been fictionalized. Several clients agreed to allow their artwork to be used for this book. Because of the potential for revictimization that comes with any request to publicly share private material, I asked only clients who were no longer seeing me as a primary therapist. The art of individuals who have experienced trauma has the potential to be morbid or shocking and, therefore, traumatizing to the therapist. I put a great deal of thought into choosing the art for this book, ultimately deciding to include works that are less graphic. Because most of my experience is with women, who represent the majority of survivors of sexual abuse, I chose to use feminine pronouns throughout the book.

Some of the techniques in this book have been passed down from therapist to therapist. I apologize if inadvertently I have failed to credit the author of a particular technique. There exists an oral history among creative arts therapists and therapists specializing in sexual abuse. I have described some techniques that are fairly well known among these two groups but may not be familiar to therapists outside of these circles. Some of the techniques in this book were collaboratively created with clients. Many of the techniques are my own synthesis of creative therapies and are not necessarily representative of mainstream art therapies or movement therapies.

It is my hope that this book will give its readers the encouragement to develop individualized nonverbal strategies with their own clients. Each intervention described in this book may work for some clients and may not work for others. In addition, there may be times when one mode is more appropriate than another. Artwork has the advantage of creating some distance from material. On the other hand, body-oriented interventions allow for a more intense here-and-now experience. Using both modalities as part of an intervention may yield a greater sense of integration. The use of nonverbal modalities may assist the survivor in transforming the silence of childhood into the language of the adult. The more tools we have as therapists, the more we can help our clients find their own way and find their own voices.

BRIDGING
THE SILENCE

1

NONVERBAL MODALITIES AND SURVIVORS OF CHILDHOOD SEXUAL ABUSE

"I DON'T KNOW HOW TO say this in words . . . ," Eliza said repeatedly in our therapy sessions. And so we would sit in silence. One day I suggested she draw how she was feeling if she did not know what to say. Choosing a red marker, she filled the page with lines, curves, and slashes, drawing rapidly for a full ten minutes.

As she described how her picture looked to her and chose adjectives that characterized the images on the page, Eliza was finally able to gain access to the anger that had been bottled up inside. We both felt that we had discovered a bridge from her silence to her words. Until describing her drawing in therapy, Eliza had never expressed her feelings of anger in words before. In fact, she initially conceived of talking about her "anger" as a foreign language that she had never learned. As a survivor of childhood sexual abuse, Eliza had experienced so many obstacles to verbalizing her feelings that she found it impossible to connect not only with her anger but with *any* feelings.

For adult survivors of childhood sexual abuse, the nonverbal modalities of art and movement can serve as a bridge between the unspoken and the spoken, between the unknown and the known, between the unconscious and the conscious. Not only do adult survivors present particular dynamics and symptoms that suggest the use of nonverbal modalities in psychotherapy but many survivors resonate deeply with nonverbal modalities, often initiating their use in therapy.

Why Is It So Hard to Talk?

Silence and Secrecy

Enduring silence around important issues is a common experience for adult survivors of childhood sexual abuse. According to Summit's (1983) theory of child abuse accommodation syndrome, secrecy is a compelling reality for the abused child enforced by the perpetrator's intimidation and by the adult conspiracy of silence and disbelief. The child is afraid to tell for fear of retaliation by the perpetrator or of punishment or dismissal by adults in the environment.

> The secret takes on magical, monstrous proportions for the child. The average child never asks and never tells. Unless the victim can find some permission and power to share the secret and unless there is the possibility of an engaging, non-punitive response to disclosure, the child is likely to spend a lifetime in what comes to be a self-imposed exile from intimacy, trust and self-validation. (Summit, 1983, pp. 181–182)

The childhood injunction of silence lives on into adulthood. As one client told me, she habitually kept her thoughts and experiences to herself; it did not even occur to her that she could talk about her inner life or her daily experiences.

The therapist of the adult survivor must build not only an empowering, trusting relationship but also an atmosphere in which secrets can be shared. Further, the therapist must help the survivor break through barriers that have long protected the magical, monstrous secrets of childhood from verbal expression. A major task in therapy is the transformation of the silence of childhood into the language of the adult.

The lack of trust that has haunted the survivor since the early betrayal by the perpetrator may impede her ability to verbalize. She is fearful that she may be disbelieved or rejected for revealing her feelings and for telling her story. According to Lister (1982), the forced silence of trauma victims results in an indirect expression of traumatic material in the form of unconscious clues. The therapist is placed in the position of a caring parent who notices the clues, unlike the abandoning or unprotective parent of the victim's childhood.

The Loss of Voice

"Voice is an indicator of self. Speaking one's feelings and thoughts is part of creating, maintaining, and recreating one's authentic self" (Jack, 1991, p. 32). Dana Crowley Jack found that depressed women experience a loss of self and voice. The authentic self is stifled by doubting her own experience, by trying to fit into others' images of who she should be, by fear of causing conflict, and by fear that she is wrong. Many survivors of sexual abuse experience the loss of self and voice described by Jack, leading to depression, low self-esteem, and an inability to verbalize thoughts and feelings. Nonverbal methods may provide the first contact with the authentic self. Alice Miller (1981) described such an experience with spontaneous painting, which gave her access to an abusive childhood by allowing "the truth to break through" (p. xiii) the constraints of her upbringing and training.

In studying women's ways of knowing, Belenky, Clinchy, Goldberger, and Tarule (1986) found that silence is a position held by women who grew up in isolation, are passive, reactive, and dependent, and see authorities as all-powerful. These women feel voiceless and have experienced words as a means to diminish and separate people. It would appear that many survivors of childhood abuse fall into the category of silent women. Belenky et al. also discovered that:

> Because the women have relatively underdeveloped representational thought, the ways of knowing are limited to the present (not the past or the future); to the actual (not the imaginary and the metaphorical); to the concrete (not the deduced or the induced); to the specific (not the generalized or the contextualized); and to behaviors actually enacted (not values and motives entertained). (pp. 26–27)

In providing concrete, here-and-now experiences, nonverbal modalities offer the means for survivors to begin to safely find their voices. Through drawing, for instance, survivors begin to break the silence without yet taking the risk of using words. Many survivors are unable to talk about their experiences of abuse but are able to draw about them. Artwork also provides an outlet for expressing feelings which the survivor may lack the verbal language to describe. Eliza, the client described above, had never put a name to what she was feeling. Her drawing provided a concrete, visual description of her feelings; seeing the intensity of her drawing and identifying the color red, she was able to begin to give a name to the anger she was feeling.

Before this episode Eliza and I had sat in silence for three sessions. By valuing the act of sitting with her without the need for words, I was able to accept her silence. During such times it is important to remember the communicative value of nonverbal behaviors, such as eye contact, postures, gestures, and breathing, which give the therapist cues into the survivor's inner world. I observed Eliza's body language gradually change from a closed, protective posture—head down, arms tightly linked around her legs, which were pulled up close to her chest—to a more open, relaxed posture—legs crossed at the knees and head up, so that her eyes occasionally met mine. Although she was unable to tell me, I knew that Eliza was beginning to feel safer with me, and so I felt I could ask her to try drawing how she was feeling.

The Defenses

Some survivors live in a metaphoric silence expressed by polished verbal proficiency reflecting highly intellectualized defenses. Words, although skillfully employed, say little about real inner thoughts and feelings. Language is a protective shield against the possibility of rejection, hurt, or exposure that intimacy has brought in the past. Drawings and body movement can open a window onto the true self, which has been hidden since childhood.

Survivors have developed many protective defenses for the sake of survival. Although the defenses may no longer be serving their original purpose and may in fact be getting in the way of healthy functioning, they need to be honored and respected. Survivors have become just that—survivors—because of the protective strategies created in childhood.

Among the many barriers that protect the survivor from the terrors of the past are the defenses of repression and denial. "The adult victim of incest wants to avoid the anxiety of remembering; she wishes to forget the trauma and push it into the past" (Blake-White & Kline, 1985, p. 396). The external pressures that reinforce silence during childhood are accompanied by internal pressures to distance the self from the knowledge of the childhood trauma, further removing the material from the verbal realm. The nonverbal modalities of art (Jung, 1952; Naumburg, 1966) and movement (Deutch, 1947; Kestenberg, 1975; Kramer & Akhtar, 1992; Reich, 1949) express the unconscious, offering a means of interpreting the disguised language of traumatic secrets.

The adult survivor may possess an inner life different from that of adult clients who did not experience childhood traumas. Isolated yet needing to make sense of betrayal by adults, the survivor carries into adulthood the child's inner life, rich with idiosyncratic symbols, magical thinking, and beliefs created in an effort to make meaning of the abusive experiences. The symbolic aspects of the survivor's inner world may be more accessible through nonverbal modes than through verbal modes.

Regressive Nature of Recalling Abuse

Another factor contributing to the lack of access to verbal language is the regressive nature of recalling the abusive experience. Survivors may not only feel overwhelmed by affects triggered by traumatic memories but also be so involved in recall of traumatic material that they regress to the immature cognitive state of the abused child, who had no repertoire of verbal language to describe the abusive experience. If abuse occurred preverbally, there may be no verbal memory from which to reconstruct the abusive event. Through the nonverbal modalities of art and movement, the survivor may find a means of expressing that to which no words have been attached. The preverbal child, who lacks the ability to use verbal language, knows how to draw and to move.

Guilt and Shame

One client said to me, "How can I talk about it [the abuse]? To talk about it is to accept that it happened. To talk about it is to betray my family. If I accept that it happened, if it is really true, then it must be my fault."

One way that the child is able to make sense of the abuse is to blame herself. The child needs to believe that the world is a just place and that adults are good people (Lerner, 1980). Within the context of this way of thinking, the child believes that she caused the abuse.

Although taking responsibility for the abuse gives the survivor a false sense of control, the process of absolving the self can be long and arduous. Because nonverbal modes have advantages over verbal ones in bypassing guilt and shame (Kreuger, 1990), they provide an avenue for assisting the survivor in viewing herself as innocent and helpless at the time of the abuse and in recognizing that she is not to blame.

The Aftereffects of Child Sexual Abuse

Every survivor responds to the trauma of child sexual abuse in her own way. The severity of symptoms in adulthood is dependent on the interaction of a number of factors, including the severity of abuse, type of abuse, chronicity of abuse, relationship of the perpetrator to the child, age of the child at the time of abuse, family climate, personality of the child, support system, and the result of efforts to disclose (Courtois, 1988; Gil, 1988). In reviewing the research on the aftereffects of child sexual abuse in 1986, Browne and Finkelhor found:

> Frequently reported long-term effects include depression, anger and hostility, aggression, and self-destructive behavior, anxiety, feelings of isolation and stigma, poor self-esteem, difficulty in trusting others, a tendency toward revictimization, substance abuse, and sexual maladjustment. (p. 66)

Browne and Finkelhor concluded that under one-fifth of victims studied evidenced severe psychopathology. Yet their findings suggest the wide range of symptom severity, impairment, and personality structure that the therapist treating adult survivors is likely to encounter.

Symptoms of Post-traumatic Stress Disorder

Many survivors experience symptoms of post-traumatic stress disorder (PTSD). In response to the experience of an overwhelming life event, PTSD symptoms range from those that flood the survivor with thoughts and feelings associated with the trauma to those that numb her to all experiences. Flooding symptoms include flashbacks and nightmares. Numbing symptoms include dissociation, amnesia or memory loss, restriction of affect, withdrawal, and loss of interest in daily events. In addition, the survivor may experience other distressing symptoms as part of a posttraumatic response, such as sleep disturbances, concentration problems, irrational guilt, hyperarousal, anxiety, and an increase of symptomatology when exposed to events similar to the original trauma (APA, 1987, 1993).

For the survivor experiencing flashbacks, there may be no words to describe the visual imagery or bodily sensations of intrusive traumatic flashbacks. Flashbacks can literally be flashes of light, color, or physical sensations (Briere & Courtois, 1992), which may be overwhelming, terrifying, or simply be indescribable. Flashbacks consisting of abstract images may be the result of a trauma that occurred preverbally or of a small part of traumatic memory leaking through into immediate recall.

Horowitz (1978) explains the route that the original traumatic experience takes to became an intrusive flashback. The mind has three cognitive modes: imagery, lexical, and enactive. The imagery mode contains visual, auditory, kinesthetic, gustatory, and olfactory imagery. The lexical mode contains words and verbal abilities. The enactive mode consists of body movement, psychosomatic symptoms, muscular activity, and nonverbal behavior.

Traumatic material is most likely to be stored as imagery in short-term memory until it is fully processed. Traumatic imagery is encoded in all sensory forms, such as the olfactory imagery of smelling a perpetrator's cologne and the kinesthetic imagery of feeling the abuse actually happening on a physical level, often referred to as body memories. Traumatic imagery is actively intrusive as long as it is stored in short-term memory. Full processing of the traumatic imagery involves translation into words and codification into long-term memory storage (Horowitz, 1978).

At the same time that survivors experience intrusive imagery, they may simultaneously experience amnesia to traumatic events or part of the events (Gelinas, 1983; Greenberg & van der Kolk, 1987; Herman, 1992; Herman & Schatzow, 1987). Such traumatic memories are more likely to be retrieved in the mode in which they are stored than in other modes (Greenberg & van der Kolk, 1987; Howard, 1990). Consequently, drawings and body-oriented interventions are excellent means to retrieve visual imagery and kinesthetic imagery, the most commonly encountered kind of traumatic imagery. As will be discussed in more detail in Chapter 2, retrieval of traumatic memories is an important step in processing the trauma.

Another aspect of traumatic memory involves the enactive mode. For the survivor of sexual abuse, this takes the form of reenactment, hyperarousal, and somaticization. Reenactment occurs through sexual promiscuity, revictimization, and abusive or unhealthy relationships (Meiselman, 1990). Often the survivor appears to be reenacting when she has actually dissociated in situations reminiscent of the original trauma, causing her to lose awareness of important cues of impending danger (Dolan, 1991). Dissociation may be curtailed through teaching the survivor to focus on sensory information in the environment. Ultimately, the survivor needs to feel safe being present in the here and now in an adult body in order to be able to stay in her body rather than disconnect from it.

Hyperarousal includes difficulty falling or staying asleep, irritability or angry outbursts, difficulty concentrating, hypervigilance, increased startle response, and physiologic reactions when exposed to events resembling the traumatic experience (APA, 1987). Relaxation exercises and regular exercise will provide the survivor with a biologically-based means to counter the physiologic intensity of hyperarousal (Flannery, 1987).

Many survivors have somatic symptoms, including gastrointestinal and respiratory problems related to the locus of assault, nausea, gagging, vomiting, and choking (Courtois, 1988; Gil, 1988). Such somaticization reflects how far from the verbal mode the reaction to the abuse has fled. Nonverbal modes allow greater access to working with somaticized symptoms and may facilitate reconnection of the somatic symptom with the original abuse experience. Somatic symptoms are characteristic of alexithymia, "the incapacity to give symbolic/linguistic representations to internal affective states" (Greenberg & van der Kolk, 1987, p. 193), which occurs as a result of infantile trauma (Krystal, 1979). It has been suggested that alexithymic individuals do not do well with verbal psychotherapy but may be able to retrieve and work through traumatic material through nonverbal modalities (Greenberg & van der Kolk, 1987).

Dissociation and Alienation from the Body

Sexual abuse is a trauma to the body that alters the survivor's relationship with the physical self. Many survivors experience an alienation or disconnection from the body (Blume, 1990; Westerlund, 1992). It is not uncommon for a survivor to describe "being in my head all the time." Intellectualization is a defense that assists the survivor in remaining distant from the body. Physical sensations and emotional feelings are beyond the perceptual range of the survivor who has disconnected body from mind. Some survivors run themselves to exhaustion because they are so out of touch with their physical selves. They forget to eat or sleep. Other survivors revile their bodies and feel they do not deserve to eat or have any physical comforts. The body may literally be a battleground, resulting in symptoms such as eating disorders and self-mutilation. The need to numb both body and mind may take the form of substance abuse.

Originally an adaptive response to the trauma, dissociation allows the child to leave the abusive experience: although the body remains present, the mind goes elsewhere. As the child matures, the dissociative response generalizes so that the adult survivor may have unpredictable incidents of spacing out, numbing, depersonalization, or amnesia (Briere, 1989). Healing from childhood sexual abuse requires that the survivor learn to be present in the here and now. In other words, the mind and body become connected. In order to connect to the body, the survivor will need to become attentive to the body, to feel safe in having a body, to learn how to be present in the body as an adult, and to feel feelings from which the survivor has long maintained psychological distance through numbing.

For many, because the trauma occurred in early childhood, the split between body and mind occurred at a young age, resulting in a lack of adult self-nurturing skills. The sexual nature of the trauma may affect how the survivor experiences sexual feelings and how the survivor views sexuality.

The impact of sexual trauma on the body demands that the body itself be a major topic at some point in treatment. Reconnecting with the body, learning how to care for the body, developing more positive feelings for the body, and recreating sexuality must occur in the process of healing. This means that the therapist must be prepared to assist the survivor in healing the body, a task that is enhanced by nonverbal modalities.

Fit of Nonverbal Modalities with Survivors' Needs

Nonverbal modalities enable clients to continue the work of therapy by undertaking art or movement tasks outside the therapy sessions (Cohen, 1992). For many clients, one or two hours per week in outpatient therapy is just not enough. The judicious use of nonverbal modalities as homework assignments, coping strategies, and transitional objects can expand the work of therapy to support the needs of the client.

In fact, many survivors instinctively initiate using art or exploring body-related phenomena. The therapist is, therefore, placed in the position of responding to the client's need to use nonverbal modalities. In addition, one of the most popular books for survivors, *The Courage to Heal* (Bass & Davis, 1988), describes many nonverbal techniques for survivors. It is not unusual for a survivor to arrive in therapy having tried the nonverbal techniques suggested by books for survivors, by previous therapists, or by friends who are also survivors.

Yet, it must always be remembered that each survivor is a unique individual who responds to the trauma of child sexual abuse with a unique pattern of coping skills and defenses. Although nonverbal modalities resonate with some survivors, the therapist needs to respect that some clients may be comfortable only using the verbal mode.

2

A SEQUENTIAL APPROACH
TO THERAPY

NONVERBAL MODALITIES USUALLY involve a directive intervention on the therapist's part. In determining the appropriate moment for an intervention, the therapist must consider the ego strength and defenses of the client, the tasks of the current phase of therapy, and the therapist's own realistic limitations. Nonverbal interventions may be conceptualized as aimed at one of three goals: (1) containment, (2) exploration, or (3) expression. Although any intervention is likely to contain elements of all three, the major emphasis will be on one of the three goals.

I cannot overemphasize the caution with which nonverbal interventions should be used in therapy. For example, if the therapist introduces an exercise that facilitates expression and the client actually needs to be working on containment, the client may become flooded and overwhelmed, resulting in a setback or even a flight from therapy. Understanding particular treatment tasks corresponding to each phase of therapy gives the therapist and client a context within which to decide if a given nonverbal approach has the potential to be helpful or disruptive.

Since therapy with adult survivors can often feel chaotic, a map that outlines the sequences of therapy is helpful. However, the route is rarely a straight line. The process of healing from childhood sexual abuse has been described as a spiral (Bass & Davis, 1988; Courtois, 1991; Sgroi, 1989); survivors revisit stages repeatedly in the therapy process, but with each successive revisitation there is a new perspective and new insights. Each survivor will approach each stage of therapy in her own way and in her own time.

A sequential approach suggests a series of phases in therapy ultimately leading to resolution of the sexual abuse trauma. Based on the early trauma resolution theories of Breuer and Freud (1893–95) and Janet (1889), trauma resolution involves retrieval of traumatic memories accompanied by expression of affect. The ability to revisit the trauma leads to a realignment in the survivor's view of the world, the self, and others. Obviously, much preparatory work must be done before the survivor is ready to face thoughts and feelings about the abuse that have remained inaccessible for so long. This is usually long-term work (Courtois, 1991; Dolan, 1991). Most current sequential theories describe a three-phase model with specific tasks in each phase (Courtois, 1991; Gil, 1988; Harkaway, 1991; Herman, 1992). Here I will describe those tasks; in the following chapters I will describe specific nonverbal strategies as they relate to treatment issues.

Early Phase Work

The primary tasks of the early phase of therapy are formation of a collaborative therapeutic alliance, creation of an atmosphere of safety and containment, assessment, treatment planning, crisis management, development of coping skills, and connection with a support network (Courtois, 1991; Harkaway, 1991). In order to form a collaborative therapeutic alliance, the client must make a commitment to therapy and the therapist must communicate to the client that they are working together and that the client's needs are important. By educating the client about the long-term effects of sexual abuse, the therapist helps to empower the client. An atmosphere of safety is created through the therapist's consistency in keeping appointments, in beginning and ending sessions on time, and in setting clear limits about fees, communication outside of scheduled appointments, and physical contact. Since trust is a major issue for survivors, the therapist needs to create a nonjudgmental atmosphere in which a trusting relationship can develop. The survivor will continually test the therapist's trust. The therapist's ability to respond consistently, fairly, empathically, and professionally will lay the groundwork for an effective therapeutic relationship.

The initial phase of therapy is a time for evaluation and history-taking. In addition to the therapist's informal assessment of the client, there are formal tools for assessment, such as the Dissociative Experiences Scale (Bernstein & Putnam, 1986), symptom checklists (Blume, 1990; Briere, 1989), and topical question lists (Gil, 1988). Drawings and nonverbal behavior may enrich the assessment process; nonverbal interventions aimed at containment are indicated at this time.

Treatment planning is a collaborative effort between client and therapist. The client comes into therapy wanting something: to remember, to feel better, to end an unhealthy relationship. Survivors often come into treatment with vague goals, unrealistic goals, or unreasonable expectations as to how long it may take to reach certain goals. It is not unusual to hear a survivor demand upon entering therapy, "I want to get this over with." Part of the treatment planning process involves the therapist's instilling hope while helping the client to formulate realistic goals. Treatment goals may change as the therapy unfolds.

Because many survivors enter therapy in crisis, a major focus may be crisis management. Nonverbal interventions aimed at containment are used at this time. If the crisis is life-threatening, a more containing environment, such as a hospital, may be warranted.

Because many survivors remain locked into using maladaptive coping skills that they first learned as children, the development of healthier coping skills is also a major focus of the first phase of therapy. Maladaptive coping behaviors, such as eating disorders, self-mutilation, substance abuse, and workaholism are not unusual. It is important to respect the client's ways of coping, with the understanding that she did the best that she could under the stressful circumstances of her life. The therapist needs to nonjudgmentally make suggestions as to how the survivor can more effectively cope. Initially, it can be quite difficult for the survivor to try a new way of coping, especially during crises. As she learns to manage stress more effectively, to recognize and tolerate feelings, to take care of herself, and to seek out nurturing relationships, nonverbal interventions may begin to focus on expression. Often these are combined with containment strategies. For instance, a survivor may draw in order to contain her self-destructive impulses at the same time that the drawing is expressing some of the affect associated with the desire to hurt herself.

A support network will assist the survivor in forming more nurturing relationships and establishing a sense of connection with others. The survivor may choose to join a therapy group, an incest survivors anonymous group (ISA), or another 12-step group, and to reevaluate current friends in order to cultivate those who are most supportive.

The length of time needed to navigate the early phase of therapy varies from survivor to survivor, depending on the ego strength of the client and the stability of her life circumstances. While some survivors may proceed to middle phase work in a matter of months, some may need years. When working with the more damaged client who may progress slowly, a mental review of early phase tasks may help the therapist maintain a sense of perspective while pacing the treatment accordingly.

Middle Phase Work

Middle phase work involves accessing traumatic memories, connecting affect with the memories (Courtois, 1991), and making new meaning out of the trauma (Colrain & Steele, 1990; McCann & Pearlman, 1990). "As a general rule, uncovering of traumatic memories ought to proceed slowly and carefully with respect for the client's defenses" (Courtois, 1991, p. 56). Efforts to remember may exacerbate symptoms of post-traumatic stress disorder. The well prepared client has a wide range of adaptive coping skills with which to tolerate the symptoms and will also be willing to add more coping skills to her repertoire. If she has learned techniques with which to cope with the intrusive symptoms of PTSD, such as flashbacks and nightmares, she will be better able to use pieces of traumatic memories as the basis for more extensive remembering. Many exploratory techniques are used to access memories, including guided imagery, photographs, and drawings.

In order to associate affect with memory, the numbing symptoms of PTSD are thawed through expressive techniques, which may involve drawing, movement strategies, and role-playing. Feelings of extreme anger and grief are typically experienced during this phase. If affect tends to become overwhelming or if intrusive symptoms interfere with daily functioning, the survivor may need to plan containing and nurturing strategies to ensure safety, such as increasing the number of therapy sessions per week, not driving, or taking planned time off from work. Together, the client and therapist need to constantly evaluate whether the affect and stress from uncovering traumatic memories are at a tolerable level. The emergence of suicidality or serious self-harm may require a postponement of memory work, although sometimes this work can be done in the safety of a hospital.

The revisiting of the trauma can lead to new learning about the abusive experience. Often the survivor discovers that she was not at fault or that there was nothing she could have done to stop the abuse. Accompanying the realization that the survivor was not responsible for the abuse is the awful, profound grief over the reality that the abuse actually happened and that adults in the victim's world perpetrated such cruel and inhumane treatment upon her. Finally, many survivors may feel intense rage at their perpetrators, while some will feel forgiveness or a combination of the two. The survivor may also struggle with whether to disclose to family members and/or whether to confront the perpetrator at this stage.

Resolution of the trauma takes place when the abuse is no longer controlling the survivor's life. Some indications that the client has reached resolution are: (1) She can manage PTSD symptoms when they arise; (2) she can discuss the trauma with affect that is neither unendurably intense nor completely absent; (3) she can respond to present events without confusing them with the past, or she can readily identify such confusion; and (4) she recognizes that she was not to blame. The client also needs to realize that there will be no magical erasure of the trauma, realistically accepting that she may continue to experience its aftereffects. As discussed above, survivors often revisit the stages of healing, armed with new resources and insights.

Because middle phase work is frequently planned, it is usually shorter than the early phase. However, trauma resolution may be interspersed with ego strengthening activities and other early phase tasks. At times middle and late phase tasks may appear to blend together; the energy and self-confidence instilled by late phase work may empower the survivor to do further work on the trauma.

Late Phase Work

Once the trauma has been resolved, the survivor can attend to other issues. Possessing a new sense of self, the survivor can be more effective in working on relational difficulties, sexuality, and symptoms such as eating disorders, depression, and anxiety (Courtois, 1991). Although the survivor has focused on many of these issues earlier in therapy, resolution of the sexual abuse trauma provides a greater sense of energy with which to address issues. Lifestyle changes may be made at this time (Herman, 1992): The survivor may quit smoking, improve her diet, or embark on an exercise program. Often vocational goals are clarified; perhaps for the first time the survivor may develop a clear picture of what she wants to do with her life. Other efforts to solidify a sense of self include assertiveness training and self-expressive exercises. The survivor may begin not only to explore ways to have fun in her daily life but also to formulate plans for the future. With the resolution of the trauma comes the ability to have more positive expectations.

Preparing for the future means preparing for the termination of therapy. The survivor should be given many weeks with which to process the meaning of leaving therapy, as feelings of loss may be intense. Dolan (1991) and Courtois (1988) recommend preparing for the possibility of relapse. The survivor may plan how she will cope with crises once therapy has ended. The client may return for periodic sessions, such as once every six months, or she may be invited to return to therapy if she feels the need to do so. Whatever termination agreement is made, the therapist needs to continue to maintain clear boundaries after termination (Courtois, 1988; Dolan, 1991).

The length of the final phase depends on the resources and needs of the client. While some survivors seem eager to be without therapy perhaps for the first time in years, others welcome the opportunity to focus in therapy on personal growth rather than abuse. Sadly, limitations on mental health coverage often prevent clients from not only completing late phase work but also resolving the trauma of sexual abuse.

A sequential approach to treatment provides a context within which the therapist can evaluate the appropriateness of a particular nonverbal intervention. As will be discussed in the next chapter in more detail, some nonverbal interventions are extremely stimulating and may invite regression if the client does not have the coping skills with which to handle the intense affect triggered by the material elicited. Based on a client's progress in the treatment tasks delineated by a sequential approach, the therapist determines whether containment, exploration, or expression is an appropriate goal and chooses nonverbal interventions accordingly.

3

FUNDAMENTALS OF ART
AND BODY-CENTERED
INTERVENTIONS

THIS CHAPTER IS DESIGNED to give the nonspecialist therapist a way to conceptualize both art and body-centered interventions in therapy with adult survivors. It will also provide some
practical information to set the stage for the safe implementation
of nonverbal interventions.

The use of art in therapy has become somewhat accepted. Since
several drawing tasks are part of the standard psychological test-
ing battery typically administered by psychologists (Lubin, Larsen,
Reed, & Mattarazzo, 1984), most clinicians are familiar with art
as an assessment tool and as a mode of expression not only for
children but also for adults. In fact, the mainstreaming of art into
psychotherapy has led several therapists to urge caution upon the
nonspecialized therapist (Cohen, 1992a; Frye & Gannon, 1990).

Movement and body-centered interventions have not yet been
generally recognized as an integrated part of psychotherapy (Kramer
& Akhtar, 1992). Interpretation of body language and expressive
body-centered techniques have for the most part remained the
realm of specialists, such as dance/movement therapists, psycho-
dramatists, and gestalt-trained therapists. Yet any therapist seeing
abuse survivors will find advantages to increasing her repertoire
to include body-centered strategies.

The Body in Psychotherapy with Adult Survivors

Sigmund Freud (1905) himself recognized the relationship between the body and the mind:

He that has eyes to see and ears to hear may convince himself that no mortal can keep a secret. If the lips are silent, he chatters with his finger tips, betrayal oozes out of him at every pore. And thus the task of making conscious the most hidden recesses of the mind is one which it is quite possible to accomplish. (Freud, 1905, pp. 77–78)

Freud saw that body language reflected unconscious psychological processes. However, he did not elaborate upon how to interpret the body's messages from the unconscious. Later Wilhelm Reich (1949), a psychoanalyst, made sense of the body's relationship to the mind by correlating psychological defenses with movement characteristics, such as chronic muscle tension and breathing patterns. He regarded specific movement patterns as reflective of particular neuroses. Trained by Reich, Alexander Lowen (1958) developed a theory called bioenergetics. Viewing muscular tension as a manifestation of emotional conflict, Lowen created body postures that evoke and release stress. Lowen is perhaps the best known advocate of integrating the body with psychotherapy.

Several systems have been developed by dance/movement therapists to correlate personality characteristics with movement patterns (Davis, 1981; Kestenberg, 1975; North, 1972), and of late there have been increasing efforts to validate such systems. Kestenberg's (1975) system integrates developmental psychoanalytic theory and object relations theory. Davis (1966, 1977, 1983; Davis & Hadiks, 1987) created systems for studying patterns of movement in the individual as well as patterns of movement interaction in families, small groups, and individual psychotherapy.

The field of movement therapy has developed not only assessment tools based on movement behaviors but also a variety of theoretical approaches to using movement as the primary means of intervention in therapy. Movement therapy emerged with two different emphases: one on the East Coast and one on the West Coast (Levy, 1988). The first movement therapist, Marion Chace (Schmais, 1974), developed a group approach using rhythm, music, and movement for back ward psychiatric patients at St. Elizabeth's Hospital in Washington. The evolution of movement therapy on the East Coast continued with a group approach aimed primarily at psychiatric patients. Meanwhile movement therapy on the West Coast developed primarily with normal and neurotic individuals. Today, there are psychoanalytic, Jungian, gestalt, humanistic, and eclectic orientations to using movement in psychotherapy. The unifying premise of movement therapy, also called dance therapy, is that "body movement reflects inner emotional states and changes in movement behavior can reflect changes in the psyche" (Levy, 1988, p. 1).

Drawing on a blend of therapeutic orientations, my approach to integrating body-oriented interventions into psychotherapy with adult survivors is grounded in the need to maintain safety in the therapeutic relationship. For this reason, the interventions that I describe will not involve the therapist moving with the client, a method generally utilized by movement therapists. I take this approach for two reasons. First, in order for the therapist to move with the client, the therapist needs substantial training in making interventions based on the client's movements rather than the therapist's own movement propensities. Such training requires hands-on experience and is far beyond the scope of what any book could provide. Second, it is assumed that most of the therapy will be verbally oriented, with nonverbal modalities being used at appropriate junctures in the therapy and according to the needs of each individual client. In such situations, if the therapist were to move with the client, this might alter the client's transference, which has thus far been based on a verbal relationship. Were the therapist to begin *moving* with the client rather than *sitting* with the client, the client would lose the predictability and boundary limitations provided by the seated relationship. Even if the therapist is a trained dance or movement therapist, the potential effects of changing the dynamics of the relationship need to be carefully considered. Shifting between moving with the client and talking with her is most easily accomplished if the therapy begins with a primarily movement-oriented approach.

Four types of body-oriented interventions are described below: (1) identification of naturalistic movement, (2) interventions that elicit naturalistic movement, (3) imposed movement exercises, and (4) exploration of body-felt sense.

Naturalistic Movement

Naturalistic describes any movements, gestures, or postures that are produced by the client and appear to belong to the client's own movement repertoire. Naturalistic movement encompasses what has come to be popularly known as body language (Fast, 1970). Movement therapists have developed several systems for describing body postures, gestures, and movements. Although such systems are much too complex for the nonspecialist therapist, some of the more obvious nonverbal indicators may be identified and integrated into therapy.

The posture that a client takes when sitting in a therapy session would be considered naturalistic movement. When the client is confronted with some aspect of traumatic memory, a dissociative reaction may be reflected in a body posture: for example, eyes may close, legs may be pulled up and tucked close to the body with arms wrapped around them, and the head may be resting on the knees, creating a seated equivalent of a fetal position.

Naturalistic movement gives the therapist information for assessment purposes; in addition, it may also be used by the client to gain knowledge about herself. In therapy, the client may emit a sigh, hold her breath, make a face, or abruptly change posture as an indication of an affect of which she is unaware. The therapist's description of the client's nonverbal behaviors in the session may help the client to gain a deeper understanding of herself. Developing an awareness of postures and gestures may also help the client in gaining some control over dissociation, a task that may be undertaken early in therapy (see Chapter 5).

The client may present a nonverbal message that is incongruent with her own self-concept. For example, a client who presents as overly seductive may have no idea that she has a sexualized body posture, or a client who is often ignored may not realize that she gives nonverbal messages through her postures and gestures that she wants to be invisible. Generally, helping the client to gain a sense of congruence between body postures and self-concept is middle- to late-stage work and requires a solid therapeutic relationship so that the client can hear the therapist's descriptions of nonverbal behavior as helpful information rather than as criticism. Additionally, the therapist needs to use great caution in bringing nonverbal behavior to the client's attention. Not only must the therapist guard against leading the client to feel that she has secret knowledge about her, but the therapist should decide "what kinds of data need to be used and what kinds need to be defended against" (Dulicai, 1976, p. 11).

Interventions that Elicit Naturalistic Movement

Many of the body-centered interventions introduced in the rest of the book are aimed at eliciting naturalistic movements from the client. These interventions are focused on bringing the client's awareness into the body so that she reacts through a movement or a posture. Before the therapist can make interventions that elicit naturalistic movement, the client must not only be ready to get in touch with her body but also feel enough trust in the therapist that she will not be too embarrassed to move or take on a body posture in front of the therapist. Examples of interventions that elicit naturalistic movement are problem-solving (Chapter 9) and anchoring adult body postures (Chapter 7), techniques that are loosely based on a gestalt orientation (Perls, Hefferline, & Goodman, 1977). In such interventions the therapist asks the client to exaggerate a movement/posture or make a movement/posture that expresses a particular feeling or experience. The externalization of internal states through nonverbal expression can lead to a greater sense of self-awareness and integration.

Imposed Movement Exercises

In imposed movement a particular set of preconceived movements is assumed by the client. Relaxation exercises and flashback strategies are examples of imposed movement exercises (see Chapter 5). Introducing an imposed movement exercise requires that a therapeutic relationship has been established, that the client has a certain degree of motivation, and that control issues are not problematic. The client must be ready to trust the therapist's suggestion to try an exercise. In introducing any kind of body-centered information or intervention, the therapist must be sensitive to the extreme sense of shame that many survivors feel in relation to their bodies.

Exploration of Body-Felt Sense

The term "body-felt sense," originated by Gendlin (1978), describes the inner sensations of the body that accompany emotional experience. Many survivors are disconnected from their internal body experience. This separation of body and mind protected the survivor not only from the sensations that were caused by the abusive incidents, but also from the intensity of affect that may have accompanied such experiences. As an adult, however, the cut-off from the body-felt sense denies the survivor the opportunity to experience emotion fully and to develop self care skills. For example, the emotion of anger may increase muscle tension and body temperature; the failure to recognize these bodily manifestations often leads to the inability to recognize not just anger, but all feelings. The ability to detect and discriminate feelings is increased by attending to the body-felt sense (Dosamantes-Alperson, 1981).

Another result of the disconnection is that the survivor's bodily experience remains locked in childhood. An awareness of the body-felt sense allows the survivor to discover her adult self, giving her the means to stay grounded in the present rather than being pulled into the past. In addition, an exploration of the body-felt sense "allows clients the opportunity to re-experience incompleted significant personal experiences which became frozen in time, to discover their current effects on their lives and to re-examine them from a fresh perspective" (Dosamantes-Alperson, 1981, p. 269). This exploration of the body-felt sense leads to the integration of body and mind that is a necessary part of healing from sexual abuse. Chapter 8 provides techniques for working with the body-felt sense.

The Role of Touch

The integration of body-centered interventions into psychotherapy may bring about a greater awareness of the physical self on the part of the survivor. Given the survivor's history of victimization and loss of control concerning her body, it is essential that the therapist respect the survivor's body boundaries and be responsible for the maintenance of limits and boundaries. Holroyd and Brodsky's (1977, 1980) research suggests that there is a relationship between a therapist's use of touch in therapy and sexual involvement with clients. It has also been suggested that sexual abuse survivors are at greater risk for sexual exploitation by therapists (Kluft, 1990). The implications of these findings support the most conservative use of touch in therapy with sexual abuse survivors. Given that we do not always know which client is a survivor, it is best to use a conservative approach with *all* clients.

A client should be touched only if the therapist has carefully weighed the therapeutic value of touch and determined that it would benefit the client. Touch should be used sparingly, only in certain situations, and with the client's permission. Each client and each situation should be evaluated. A client who tests the therapist's limits, is seductive, or is experiencing an erotic transference should not be touched. Generally, touch may be appropriate during abreactions, memory work, and intense grief reactions. At those times, the therapist may ask the client if she would like to hold her hand. Gil (1991) has suggested telling the client, "My hand is here if you want to hold it," thus presenting the client with a real choice.

I may move my chair closer to the client or sit beside her during intense or stressful moments in the therapy. When there is doubt about whether to touch the client, the therapist should err on the side of caution.

Milakovich's (1992) study of touch in psychotherapy found that a substantial number of therapists touch their clients and that therapists' use of touching stemmed from two basic motivations: the therapist's personal style, and his/her theoretical understanding of the client's difficulties. One unexpected finding of the study was that therapists who themselves did not experience sexual abuse were less likely to touch their clients than those who did.

Obviously, survivors need to experience touch in a safe, nonsexualized manner. However, the paramount importance of creating a safe, collaborative therapeutic relationship often makes touch in therapy off limits. The therapist is challenged to help the survivor reframe the meaning of touch without touching the client.

Art in Psychotherapy with Adult Survivors

The use of art in therapy has its roots in the thinking of Freud (1915) and Jung (1952). Freud introduced the idea that imagery is an expression of the unconscious as depicted in dreams, while Jung made the more direct connection between imagery in art and the symbolic language of the unconscious.

Margaret Naumberg (1966), who was trained in psychoanalytic theory, pioneered the use of art in therapy, using spontaneous drawings as a means to elicit free association and to interpret conflicts as seen in the symbolic meaning of art images. Another approach was taken by Edith Kramer (1971), who believed that the process of creating art is a healing experience unto itself and verbal processing is not necessary.

Naumberg and Kramer represent the polarity in orientations which has emerged in the field of art therapy, with one approach focusing on the art and the other focusing on the therapy (Wadeson, 1980). The term art psychotherapy (Lusebrink, 1990) has been used to differentiate the approach which focuses on the therapy: "The emphasis is placed upon the *process* of creating the expression, and the client's verbalization about the visual product integrates its different aspects for him/her" (Lusebrink, 1990, p. 12). Under the rubric of art therapy, various theoretical orientations have been developed, including Jungian, humanistic, and psychoanalytic perspectives.

The interventions presented in this book are drawn from a range of approaches and orientations. I concur with Levick's (1967, 1983) perspective that, regardless of the viewpoint, the goals for using art in therapy are to:

1. provide a means for strengthening the ego,
2. provide a cathartic experience,
3. provide a means to uncover anger,
4. offer an avenue to reduce guilt,
5. facilitate a task to develop impulse control,
6. introduce an experience to help develop the ability to integrate and relate,
7. help [clients] use art as a new outlet during an incapacitating [episode]. (Levick, 1983, pp. 9–10)

Like movement, art is used for assessment as well as intervention. As an assessment tool, art is seen to reflect personality traits, personality development, and unconscious conflicts (Hammer, 1978). As in movement assessments, the interpretation of drawings for the purpose of evaluation and diagnosis is beyond the scope of this text and is recommended for the trained professional. However, the nonspecialist therapist can gain useful knowledge from artwork, especially when the client provides information about the meaning of symbols and images. (See Chapter 4 for more on interpreting drawings.)

There are three types of situations in which art is encountered in psychotherapy: (1) client-initiated art, (2) art produced in the therapy session, and (3) collaborative art produced outside of the session. While the interventions described in this book are included in the last two categories, it is helpful for the therapist to have some guidelines for art that is client initiated and brought into therapy.

Client-Initiated Art

Several of my clients have brought a pile of drawings to the first few sessions, often with the simple explanation: "I thought you would want to see these." The offering of drawings by a client can parallel an early encounter with parents when the child brought home from school a drawing or a well-done assignment. For the child who lived in a dysfunctional family, such symbols of accomplishment were often ignored, ridiculed, or destroyed. In therapy, the client is trying to renegotiate such early experience with the therapist. With this in mind, the therapist should respectfully accept the client's work. I always thank clients for sharing their artwork with me and make a comment such as: "I really appreciate your showing me your drawings."

The next task is to decide if it is appropriate to process the drawings together in the session. Sometimes clients want me to look at their artwork outside the session. I usually explain that it would be more meaningful if we looked at it together. If a client brings in many drawings, I ask her to choose the drawing that has the most significance. I then simply say, "Tell me about the picture." Frye and Gannon (1990) have offered this helpful guideline:

"Ask patients to tell you about their work. Open ended questions using 'who, what, when, where, and how' are helpful. Asking 'why' usually invites intellectualization" (p. 9). I may ask the client to explain the meaning of certain objects or relationships that appear in a picture. I am interested in the client's thoughts, feelings, and associations to the drawing, as well as the conditions that led to her making the drawing. A question which may be relevant, especially when art was made in the past and brought into therapy, is "What were you thinking when you decided to bring this picture in to me?"

Whenever the client produces art, the therapist must evaluate whether the experience of creating or viewing art is overstimulating for the client. "Flooding, which can occur when too much is uncovered too quickly in therapy, may be initiated or escalated by artmaking, especially when not properly monitored" (Cohen, 1992a, p. 13). The client may need help in modulating the outflow of art and, in some cases, in deciding to discontinue the production of art. Putting the modulation of artmaking into the context of the client's taking control over the effect of the abuse in her present life may minimize her feelings of being criticized or rejected.

One way to assist the client in modulating the intensity of material uncovered through artwork is an analogy that I first heard from David Perry, Ph.D., who suggested it as a way to help clients self-monitor dreams brought into therapy:

> Bringing art into therapy is much like mountain climbing. When you first start out you want to start with the small hills and move on to the medium-sized hills before conquering the huge mountains.

A client who brings in a drawing of traumatic material early in the therapy and becomes flooded by thoughts and feelings can appreciate the analogy without feeling criticized.

The therapist is faced with a tricky situation when she has an interpretation that the client has not made herself: Should she hold her tongue or share the interpretation with the client? If the therapist feels compelled to make an interpretation, it should be offered to the client as a possibility rather than a given. First the therapist needs to consider whether the client is ready to hear the interpretation. She also needs to evaluate to what degree her own issues or biases may be influencing her interpretation. Because many survivors have difficulty verbalizing, it is sometimes helpful for the therapist to make an interpretation that seems obvious to the therapist but has not occurred to the client. However, the therapist needs to be aware that her interpretation may, in fact, be incorrect or that the client may accept the interpretation because she is highly suggestible or wants to please the therapist.

If the therapist has little experience and/or training with art interpretation, it is best to allow the client to make her own interpretations, with the therapist assisting as she clarifies her thoughts, feelings, and ideas about the picture. In other words, the therapist can summarize the client's interpretations and associations, giving them more weight and impact. It may be helpful to consult with an art therapist for diagnostic and interpretation questions.

Art Produced in the Therapy Session

Because of the limited time available in outpatient therapy, it is often not convenient for the client to make art as part of a session. However, there are several situations in which making art in the therapy session is helpful or warranted. For clients who have never used art, are motivated to do so, but feel shy or intimidated, trying the first artmaking experience with the therapist's support can facilitate increased comfort with the medium. It is important to emphasize that the purpose of drawing is not to be a good artist but to express oneself. In fact, it is not necessary to have any artistic skill or training to use art as part of psychotherapy. As the client draws in the session, the therapist can monitor her anxiety about the experience and make supportive comments. Perfectionism can be an obstacle to comfortably using art; the therapist may be able to refocus the perfectionistic client on more process-oriented aspects of artmaking rather than on the visually aesthetic quality of the work.

Another situation in which artmaking in the session may be indicated is in the case of a client who is obviously having difficulty putting thoughts and feelings into words, such as Eliza, described in Chapter 1. Sometimes a client may verbalize feeling confused or overwhelmed. One client explained to me, "I just feel all this *stuff*." She was unable to describe the "stuff" so I asked her to draw how she was feeling. A drawing allowed her to see her feelings reflected in her art images; the "stuff" took on the form of concrete images to which she was able to associate and which she translated into the feeling of anxiety, thereby gaining access to her psychological state. Generally, I prefer to allow the client to come up with her own ideas for drawings; however, if she appears stumped or blocked, especially for the first drawing, I may suggest that she draw how she is feeling using lines, shapes, and colors. If this fails, asking the client to choose a color that reflects how she is feeling seems to provide enough structure to support the production of artwork.

Art may be produced in a session when the client is working on memory retrieval. Drawing may provide a means for the expression of unspeakable traumata. Specific interventions are discussed in Chapter 11.

Collaborative Art Produced Outside the Session

As part of a collaborative therapeutic relationship, the client may produce art outside of the sessions at the therapist's suggestion or as part of a jointly agreed upon treatment plan. Many survivors need or want far more therapy than they can financially afford. "Artmaking is a powerful and economical mode that can stretch therapy hours while at home" (Cohen, 1992a, p. 13). The client and therapist may agree that the client will produce art in an ongoing way outside of the therapy sessions, or the therapist may suggest a drawing assignment based on material from a therapy session. Many of the art interventions suggested in this book can be suggested to the client as homework assignments. As discussed above, the therapist needs to evaluate whether artmaking outside the session is counterproductive for the client.

Drawing can also give the client a sense of continuity when the therapist is absent (Oster & Gould, 1987). When the therapist or the client is on vacation, the client may make drawings that communicate her experiences or use other structured art assignments for the purpose of maintaining the therapeutic connection. In these situations, the art can serve as a transitional object representing the therapist.

Supplies and Art Media

The choice of art media is based on the practical considerations of the therapy setting as well as the properties of a particular art medium. For example, in my own practice the variety of art media I can offer in my office is limited by my schedule, such that there is no time to clean up messier art media, such as paints, clay, or pastels. Among the properties of art media relevant for survivors is the degree to which the media are fluid or resistive (Cohen, 1992b; Kagan & Lusebrink, 1978; Lusebrink, 1990; Rubin, 1983). More fluid media, such as fingerpaints or clay, can invite regression. I recommend that therapists who have little training in the uses of different art media use more resistive media: chalk, oil pastels, magic markers, crayons, and pencil. It is important to have a full range of colors available. When art supplies are visibly arranged in the office, clients are more likely to use them.

The therapist and client should collaboratively decide how and where artwork should be stored; if the patient keeps her artwork, she should agree not to destroy it. However, at times the therapist and client may make a decision to destroy a certain art production for therapeutic reasons. For several reasons the therapist should consider storing clients' drawings in her office: Artwork can provide a visual record of the therapy and progress can be seen in drawings (Hammer, 1978); themes may emerge through images that appear repeatedly over time in drawings; issues reflected in drawings may re-emerge; and sometimes the meaning of an image may not be apparent until later in the therapy. Storing artwork in the office keeps it available for reintegration into therapy and prevents clients from destroying or losing it.

Figures 1, 2, and 3 show the image of a snake in drawings done over a three-year period. When the client, Joan, first drew Figure 1, she was unable to talk about sexual abuse; although the image of a snake is often associated with sexuality, Joan did not talk about the issue at the time and made no interpretation of the snake. One year later, when she drew Figure 2, she had begun to explore the possibility of having been sexually abused as a child. At this point, she tentatively interpreted the snake as a symbol of sexual abuse, but she was not sure. Another year later, when Joan was directly addressing her sexual abuse in therapy, she made a collage (Figure 3) describing her thoughts and feelings about the topic. This was the first time that the meaning of the snake in her artwork was clear to Joan. Taken together, the three drawings reflected Joan's progress in dealing with sexual abuse. At a time when Joan was feeling rather frustrated by her lack of progress in therapy, we reviewed her drawings and she was heartened to see a visual record of her progress reflected by the snake drawings.

Another approach for storing artwork is for the client to keep a sketchpad and bring it to every session. The more formal structure of the sketchpad not only provides for storage but also gives the drawings a certain importance, so the client may be less inclined to destroy them.

White paper is best, as colors are more vivid on it. Because I store a great deal of artwork, I tend to use 8½ by 11 inch white paper, which stores easily in a manilla folder in a filing cabinet. Some clients inevitably want larger paper. I have a portfolio in which I can store larger works; however, I do not like to store all my clients' works in one portfolio, as it is not always easy to remove one drawing without taking out many.

An Integrated Approach

Imagery forms the basis for many of the intervention strategies in this book. Imagery not only is the form in which traumatic memory is stored, but also provides a medium through which difficult topics may be approached and change rehearsed (Singer, 1974). Hyde and Watson (1990) described guided imagery with incest survivors as a technique that can stimulate both visual and kinesthetic imagery. The facility to implement both the visual and kinesthetic modes gives the therapist greater flexibility in adapting to the perceptual style of the client. In addition, there may be times when one mode is more appropriate than another. Artwork has the advantage of creating some distance from the material. Body-oriented interventions, on the other hand, allow for an intense, here-and-now experience. Using both modalities as part of an intervention may yield a greater sense of integration. Once the therapist develops some familiarity with using nonverbal modalities and gains experience in treating adult survivors, she may, in collaboration with the client, create individualized strategies that are uniquely suited to each client.

Figure 1

Figure 1, 2, 3   *Emergence of client's ability to confront issue of sexual abuse as seen in art over three-year period*

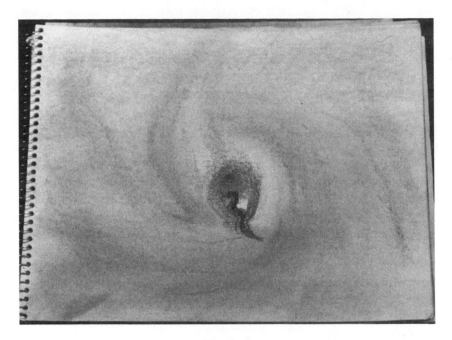

Figure 2

Figure 3

Considerations for the Therapist

Nonverbal modalities are amenable to the expression of primary process thinking, which includes the raw, uncensored memories of trauma. The therapist working with nonverbal modalities may be faced with traumatic material that is more vividly horrific than its verbal equivalent. The visual accessibility of the material may make the therapist herself more vulnerable to being traumatized by the traumatic imagery. Moreover, the vividness of traumatic imagery may create unusually compelling artwork, prompting the therapist to share clients' work with colleagues, who are then vulnerable to traumatization. Unless care is exercised, viewing artwork may lead to secondary traumatization among clinicians.

Increased sensitivity to body-related phenomena has the potential to weaken the therapist's sense of boundaries between herself and the client. When the client describes body memories, the therapist may very well feel sympathetic body sensations. When the client expresses feelings through postures or gestures, the therapist may unconsciously take on the same movements or consciously take them on in an effort to be more empathic. The result is that the therapist is vulnerable to losing her sense of self as she feels the client's emotions and traumatic memories. As the therapist sits with a highly dissociated client, she may find herself unconsciously reflecting the client's body posture, leading to her own dissociation. A similar phenomenon may operate with regard to sexualized postures. The therapist's unconscious emulation of a client's sexualized posture may lead her to experience erotic feelings. When an erotic posture is combined with a dissociative one, the therapist is more susceptible to acting out erotic feelings toward the client. Since the client may unconsciously take on the postures of those around her, the therapist is cautioned to pay attention to her own body positions and to maintain grounded, nonsexualized postures.

I have used a variety of activities to help me cope with the intensity of working with sexual abuse trauma. When a client does powerful abreactive work in a session, I try to take a brief walk outside of my office, even for less than five minutes, if I have another client scheduled directly after the abreactive session. The effort required on the part of the therapist to stay grounded during an abreaction can result in muscle tension. Physical activity, like a walk or stretching, can remove the impact of a client's traumatized body movements from the therapist's body.

I highly recommend regularly scheduled supervision meetings for those working with survivors. Regardless of the level of expertise of the therapist, a supervision meeting provides an excellent outlet and support mechanism. I also have a number of colleagues with whom I can discuss cases when I feel overwhelmed. Going to conferences and training seminars is helpful as well, although I have found that the onslaught of many hours of material on sexual abuse can be traumatizing in itself. I now either attend with a colleague so that we can deprogram ourselves during breaks, or I make sure that I do something distracting, such as go to a movie (preferably a comedy), at night.

At one time I ran a group for survivors, which proved to be particularly stressful due to the extreme fragility among the group members. After several sleepless nights immediately following the group, I instituted my own treatment plan, whereby I rented a comedy at the video store on my way home from the group. Watching the movie prevented me from ruminating about the group and helped me maintain a sense of optimism while working with a tremendously damaged group of clients. By giving me a buffer between the pain of the group and my own life, the movie truly helped me sleep better.

4

ENRICHING THE
ASSESSMENT PROCESS

ALTHOUGH THE ASSESSMENT PROCESS is an ongoing part
of the first phase of therapy, the first three to four sessions are
crucial in determining diagnosis, the fit of the client and therapist,
and realistic treatment goals. Movement behavior, also known as
nonverbal behavior, can be unobtrusively included in the therapist's information-gathering from the moment the client walks
into the office. Assessment through art is a more interactive process, the inclusion of which is dependent on the climate of the
therapy. It may be helpful to take a formal history as part of the
third or fourth session, concluding the session with a drawing
task.

I am often asked if it is possible to identify a history of childhood sexual abuse through art or movement. The little research
on movement indicators of sexual abuse has been with children
or within the particular diagnostic category of multiple personality
disorder (discussed in Chapter 10). There is more empirical research in the area of art indicators, while movement indicators
have been culled from clinical observations or case studies. Although certain art or movement indicators may raise the possibility of such a history (as certain symptoms or historical antecedents
would), childhood sexual abuse has a broad range of characteristics and aftereffects, resulting in any number of diagnostic entities
in adults. Most of the studies have used inpatients or children
in treatment programs who have severe symptomatology. Con-

sequently, efforts to identify (or rule out) a history of childhood sexual abuse through nonverbal indicators should be made with caution, especially by nonspecialist therapists. Nevertheless, some of the more prevalent characteristics cited by the research are discussed below.

Nonverbal Behavior

When the client arrives in the office for the first appointment, many clinicians take note of body-centered behavior but do not necessarily have a systematized approach for categorizing and assessing such behavior. As mentioned in Chapter 3, there are several systems developed by movement therapists to assess psychopathology based on nonverbal behavior. Although the systems are too complex for clinicians without formal movement observation training, there are several types of nonverbal behavior which the clinician may easily identify and integrate into the assessment process.

Because nonverbal behavior may express manifestations of the client's unconscious, the therapist has the advantage of identifying information about the client that is outside of the client's awareness. It is vitally important, when incorporating nonverbal behavior into the therapy process, for the therapist to carefully share information or hypotheses gleaned from such behavior, so that the client will not feel that the therapist is being critical or has secret information about her. This can be especially tricky in dealing with seductive postures and gestures. In the spirit of creating a collaborative therapy relationship, the therapist needs to help the client develop an awareness about nonverbal behavior. However, in the early phase of therapy such information may be solely for the use of the therapist, to assist in deciding whether to accept a case, to help the therapist establish rapport on a nonverbal level, or to identify ego strengths and weaknesses.

For the clinician new to incorporating nonverbal behavior into the assessment process, a checklist may be helpful (see Table 1). Each item on the checklist is discussed in more detail below. Although there are many more nonverbal indicators, the items chosen not only have particular relevance for sexual abuse survivors but also can be readily observed.

Table 1: *Nonverbal Behavior Checklist*

1. eye contact
   good
   intermittent
   none
2. proximity and boundaries
   close
   makes contact
   average
   far
   alternates between close and far
3. synchrony
   present
   absent
4. quality of self-touch
   nurturing
   self-destructive
5. sexualized postures or gestures
   present
   absent
6. open vs. closed posture
   upper body
      open
      closed
   lower body
      open
      closed
7. bizarre or seemingly random body movements
   present
   absent
8. grounded posture
   present
   absent
9. body attitude
   overall body attitude
   held areas
   passive areas
   other unusual areas

As far as I have been able to determine, no empirical studies exist which investigate the nonverbal or movement indicators of sexually abused adults. Biggins (1989) has developed a characteristic profile of nonverbal behavior for sexually abused girls based on case studies of sexually abused children (Goodill, 1987; Weltman, 1986). My clinical observations of adult women survivors' movement patterns are consistent with many of Biggins' findings.

Some of the movement variables from Biggins' work which I have frequently found in adult survivors are: poor eye contact; extreme tension in the body and chronic tension patterns; center of body disconnected from periphery; head disconnected from body; poor body boundaries; intrusiveness or need for much personal space; grounding problems; poor or distorted body image; aggressive self-directed movements; sexualized movements or postures; inability to use strong movements; little upright emphasis to body or extreme of upright emphasis.

The presence of these movement indicators does not necessarily reflect that an individual is a survivor of sexual abuse; yet they have been found to be present in sexual abuse survivors in a variety of combinations and levels of intensity. There have been no comparison studies to isolate the movement characteristics particular to sexual abuse survivors.

Lest the therapist become overwhelmed by a list in actually trying to identify nonverbal indicators during therapy, it is recommended that she concentrate on the item or items that stand out as the most unusual or characteristic. It is important to note that the presence of any one nonverbal indicator is not necessarily sufficient information for the therapist to draw a conclusion about the client. Rather, the presence of an indicator can assist the therapist in forming a hypothesis and gathering other data, both verbal and nonverbal, as support. The checklist in Table 1 is consistent with movement variables that are particular to sexual abuse survivors, is reflective of corresponding issues that are likely to emerge in the therapy, and is designed for the nonspecialist therapist with no training in movement observation.

Eye Contact

Many survivors are extremely uncomfortable making eye contact with the therapist. Clients may close their eyes or look away when talking. Often the client cannot tolerate the intimacy that eye contact creates. In other cases, the client may feel too embarrassed to look the therapist in the eye, especially while discussing material related to abusive experiences. The effect of avoiding eye contact may parallel the self-protective coping strategies that the survivor has used since childhood to avoid intimacy: Avoiding eye contact protects the survivor from seeing the rejection that she has come to expect. Paradoxically, avoiding eye contact denies the survivor the reality of the therapist's acceptance and caring.

At times, lack of eye contact is reflective of dissociative phenomena. When a client has entered an altered state, the eyes may be closed, glazed, or seemingly focused on nothing and moving slightly but rapidly. The client usually dissociates for either of two possible reasons: (1) The material being discussed has triggered traumatic imagery; or (2) the intensity of the client's affect, based either on a transference reaction or on traumatic material, has resulted in the client's needing to escape through dissociation.

Usually around the middle phase of therapy, the therapist and client can work on identifying the reasons for the client's lack of eye contact. When dissociation is the reason, the client may be able to work on eye contact as part of learning coping skills to stay grounded. If relationship issues are impeding eye contact, this may be an issue better addressed later in therapy.

Gina initiated a discussion of her lack of eye contact in the late phase of therapy, explaining that it was a treatment goal of hers to be able to look at me during the session. A painful discussion about what she would see if she looked at me revealed that Gina expected rejection, just as she had been rejected by her grandmother, who was her caretaker. This assisted Gina in differentiating past relationships from present ones; ultimately she was able to look at me during therapy sessions. Gina was able to understand that she lost the opportunity of seeing my acceptance by avoiding eye contact, and she was able to begin to risk looking at me. She found that outside of therapy she experienced greater ease in social interactions once she understood that her difficulty with eye contact was based on old expectations of rejection.

Proximity and Boundaries

Clients habitually change the location or direction of their chair in my office, even if just slightly. Gina's need for distance was reflected in her customary positioning of the chair slightly further away from me, while Laura's dependency needs were reflected in her moving the chair closer toward me, so that her feet were almost touching mine.

Other cues about proximity can be gleaned from walking in and out of the office with the client. Does the client need a lot of distance or does the client want to be close? Does this change as the dynamics in the therapy change? For instance, if a client is mad at me, she may move her chair an inch or two back from its regular spot, whereas if there is a highly positive transference or an idealized transference the client may move her chair closer. An eroticized transference may be expressed through proximity: The client may come closer in the midst of her erotic excitement or she may back off due to her discomfort.

Proximity also gives information about body boundaries and ego boundaries. Darlene repeatedly described how she could not stand to be close to her former male therapist, reflecting her need for distinct body boundaries. However, when I walked her into my office, she often bumped into me, reflecting permeable boundaries. Just as the survivor's family has boundaries that are too rigid or too diffuse or a combination of the two (Courtois, 1988), the survivor herself may experience extremes in boundary maintenance.

If the therapist's office has several chairs from which a client can choose, the choice may be revealing in regard to the client's need for distance or closeness. A change to a different chair is worth exploring with the client to discover how the change parallels issues in the therapy.

Synchrony

The session with Gina was going very well. As I reached up to scratch my head, I noticed that she was doing the same thing at the same time. We were experiencing empathic synchrony. Synchrony has been found to occur in social situations when one individual responds to another on a nonverbal level (Kendon, 1979). Synchrony can take the form of gestures or postures and may occur in response to words as well as body movements; a listener's finger may move in time to the talker's words even when no eye contact is being made.

When the therapist and client have established a rapport, there is a synchrony in gestures and postures that I describe as empathic. Although synchrony may be occurring in gestures, the therapist may enhance the empathic synchrony with the client by subtly mirroring the client's posture (Grinder & Bandler, 1981); this is particularly helpful in the first few sessions. For instance, in the first session, if a therapist is sitting up very tall and straight and the client is sitting slumped down in her chair, the client may subtly feel isolated, patronized, or more depressed. The therapist, by relaxing her body downward in a way that mirrors the client, may decrease the emotional distance between herself and the client. If the client is uncomfortable with even the potential for intimacy, she may shift her posture in some way to retain the distance between them, a distance that may be more ego syntonic.

When there appears to be no empathic synchrony, that is, when the client and therapist experience no or few moments of synchrony during the therapy sessions, the therapist can suspect that there is low rapport, high dissociation, fears of intimacy, or poor contact with reality.

The therapist may also glean useful information as to the client's emotional state by mirroring the client's body posture and experiencing the resulting affect. The therapist needs to be able to maintain solid boundaries when trying this technique, so as not to confuse the client's feelings with the therapist's feelings and vice versa.

Quality of Self-Touch

At her first appointment, Jean sat across from me in my office, picking at her cuticles with a quick, piercing movement. "That looks like it hurts," I said to her. "I wasn't even aware that I was doing it." Upon further questioning, Jean revealed that she had a history of cutting her upper arms and thighs with a safety pin.

Because self-mutilation is a symptom found in sexual abuse survivors (Briere, 1989; Courtois, 1988; Dolan, 1991; Gil, 1988), it is important for the therapist to assess for a history of such behavior. Most clients answer truthfully when asked; however, for some the behavior may be repressed, dissociated, or too embarrassing to discuss in the early phases of therapy. Assessing the quality of the client's self-touch gives the therapist information about the client's potential to nurture or abuse her body. For instance, most people touch themselves unconsciously with self-soothing gestures; this might be seen when an individual hugs her arms around her chest and gently rubs the hand or finger against herself. A quite different meaning can be hypothesized by the individual who hugs her arms around her chest and proceeds to grab herself tightly, to the point of pinching. In this case, the self-touch is not nurturing and may be expressing anger turned toward the self. For the survivor who is not connected with her feelings or who feels too uncomfortable to talk about herself, the quality of self-touch can shed much light on the survivor's relationship with the self.

Sexualized Postures or Gestures

Lucy sat in the chair in my office in a sexualized posture in which her chest was pulled to one side, her pelvis was thrust to the other, and her right leg was crossed over her left leg, dangling freely. She had no awareness of the sexual message her posture gave out and found herself surprised when she was propositioned by both men and women. This was a difficult topic to approach with Lucy because she became defensive and denied that she engaged in any kind of behavior that was sexualized. No amount of explanation as to the unconscious nature of postures enabled Lucy to feel more comfortable in seeing her own behavior. In this case, I was not only cued in to the extent to which Lucy's sexualized behavior was unconscious, but also made aware of her defensiveness. This information helped me develop realistic treatment expectations for Lucy; it also hinted that therapy would be a long-term process.

Open vs. Closed Posture

The body is divided into two parts: upper body and lower body. Both upper and lower body may be habitually in a closed posture, such as with arms folded and legs crossed. A closed posture may reflect anxiety about intimacy. Both the upper and lower body may be in an open posture, with arms at the sides and legs uncrossed, reflecting an invitation to intimacy. An extremely open lower body with legs open may be a sexual invitation. A closed upper torso with an open lower torso sends a mixed message about intimacy. The degree of openness or closedness of posture communicates a message to others about an individual's willingness to relate.

It is not unusual for clients to be unaware of the message their postures send to others. For instance, one client wanted desperately to make friends yet she habitually had a closed posture and felt constantly rejected in social situations.

Bizarre or Seemingly Random Body Movements

The presence of bizarre or seemingly random body movements may be a clue to the presence of dissociative phenomena or psychotic thought processes. When individuals with multiple personality disorder switch personalities, unusual movements that seem to come out of nowhere may accompany the switching process. Repetitive, ritualized movements may be reflective of an underlying thought disorder or organicity. Such movements allow the therapist to form hypotheses about the underlying problem and pursue further investigation through other evaluative tools.

Grounded Posture

A grounded posture keeps the client literally connected to the ground, which ties her to the present. An ungrounded walk can look like walking on air or on eggshells. The less grounded a client's walk is, the less likely she is to be connected to the here and now. While a style of walking is characterologic, a posture is transient; a client will exhibit many postures in a session. However, if a client takes on predominantly ungrounded postures throughout a session, the therapist may conclude that the client is having difficulty being present. Ungrounded seated postures include: legs drawn up close to the chest with feet on the chair; one or no legs touching the ground; any posture reminiscent of a fetal position. A client in an ungrounded posture is more likely to dissociate.

Body Attitude

Body attitude is descriptive of the overall shape and attitude of the entire body. For example, the body may appear tall and energetic, round and collapsed, or tense with an exaggerated upward stress. Body attitude also encompasses areas of the body where tension is held or blocked, as described by Reich's (1949) character armor. Some of the areas where survivors may appear held or blocked are the chest, shoulders, pelvis, and hands. When the tension in the chest is held or blocked, feelings of sadness may be blocked, intimacy may be conflictual, or there may be difficulties around mothering or nurturing. When the shoulders are held or collapsed, the survivor may be carrying a great burden. A held or blocked pelvis is usually reflective of sexual conflicts. When the flow of energy to the hands appears blocked or the hands appear overly invested with energy, the survivor may be experiencing intense guilt or conflict about taking action. The body attitude may change over time as the sexual abuse trauma is resolved and the client's defensive structure changes.

One way to become more adept at observing and describing the body attitude is to practice with bodies seen on television. For the untrained therapist, only unusual or pronounced body attitudes may be apparent. These will be more evident if the sound is turned off.

Drawings

In the early stages of therapy, several types of drawings can provide additional information about the client; in addition, these may serve as landmarks against which to measure growth and change produced over the course of therapy. If the client feels comfortable drawing, the therapist can request that she complete a drawing assignment either as part of the session or as homework. The therapist may gain more information if the drawing is done during a therapy session. When artwork is done out of the office, the therapist may not know how much investment the client put into producing the drawing and what external stimuli may have influenced its contents.

Sometimes it is best to hold off drawing until later in the therapy, especially if the client seems quite fragile. Drawings may elicit memories or feelings that the client is unprepared to handle. If the client shows a reluctance to draw, the therapist needs to evaluate whether the hesitation is based on trust issues, performance anxiety, or conflict over the content of the requested drawings. While the client with performance anxiety may be supported with encouragement, the client experiencing trust issues and conflict over content may need to wait until the therapy has progressed to the point that both the client and the therapist have some confidence that the client can cope with the thoughts and feelings that the drawings may elicit. If therapy progresses well, the motivated client may in later sessions be interested in trying to use drawing to learn more about herself. It is important for the therapist to recognize that many clients will be anxious about their drawing skills and will need reassurance that skill is unimportant.

If a client has strong potential for becoming flooded by drawing, I defer drawing until the client is better able to tolerate affect. Some indications that a client is vulnerable to flooding from drawing are:

1. The client reports being frequently overwhelmed or flooded with feelings or thoughts to the extent that she becomes nonfunctional, violent, suicidal, or homicidal.
2. The client refuses to talk about numerous issues, particularly family history.

Two drawings are particularly useful in the assessment process: the Kinetic Family Drawing (Burns & Kaufman, 1970) and a self portrait (Gil, 1988). While the Kinetic Family Drawing is frequently used in evaluations of children (Hammer, 1980), the self-portrait is not part of standard art evaluations. Although all drawings offer the opportunity for sophisticated analyses and diagnoses based on an understanding of technical concepts in drawings, the non-art therapist can use drawings to gain knowledge from the content of the drawings and the client's explanations and associations to them.

Kinetic Family Drawing

An understanding of the context in which the childhood abuse occurred, the dynamics of family relationships, and the role the client played in the family as a child can be enormously helpful to both the therapist and client in making sense of the transference issues that are likely to develop in the course of therapy. The more information the therapist has about the client's early exposure to relatedness and intimacy, the more likely it is that the therapist will be able to help the client untangle the past from the present. Sometimes a client cannot tolerate exploring family history in the beginning of therapy. In those cases, the client is probably revealing a need to fend off intense emotions associated with the childhood abuse, and a focus on family is best delayed. Sometimes drawing tasks must be put off until the client is doing uncovering work and is better equipped to face the potential unleashing of emotions and memories that drawings can stimulate. It is also possible to have the client complete the drawing tasks in the beginning of therapy and spend little time processing them until later in the therapy.

The instructions for the Kinetic Family Drawing (KFD) are: *Draw a picture of your family doing something together*. For the adult survivor, this instruction can be modified to:

Draw a picture of your family doing something together during your childhood.

Kaufman and Wohl (1992) note numerous aspects of the KFD which lend themselves to interpretation in the family of a sexually abused child and that can similarly be applied to the adult survivor. Some of the questions to explore with the client upon completion of the KFD are:

- How do you see yourself?
- How do you see other family members?
- How does each family member appear to use his or her body?
- Do family members appear proud or ashamed of their bodies?
- How clear are the boundaries of each family member, particularly your boundaries with regard to other family members?
- What role does each family member play?
- Who is most dominant and who is most submissive?
- What alliances and disharmonies are there among family members?
- Are you isolated or close to other family members?

- How connected do you appear to be with each parent?
- Is any family member missing?
- Does any family member appear substantially different from the rest of the family members?
- What meaning might the activity in which the family is engaged have?

Another approach is to ask the client to tell you a story about the family, including each person who appears in the drawing. Discussion of any pets that appear in the drawing is important, as many abused and neglected children experienced their most consistent, affectionate, and trusting relationship with pets; in some cases, there has been abuse or threats involving pets as well.

Eliza's KFD showed four people sitting at the dinner table with one significantly larger figure at the end of the table. There were empty plates on the table. The bodies of the figures were blobs with appendages attached as arms and legs. Eliza identified the figures as her mother, father, sister, and brother. The larger figure was her mother. When I asked Eliza why she was not in the picture, she stated, "I was probably in my room." Her mother's larger size was explained by her feeling of intimidation by her mother. My question about the meaning of drawing a mealtime scene with empty plates led Eliza to describe her family as a place where she got little nurturance. This also helped Eliza understand why mealtime with her husband and children was so stressful for her. The isolation and exclusion Eliza felt in her family continued into her adult life. As Eliza continued to work on issues of inclusion and exclusion in a therapy group for survivors, she repeatedly referred to her KFD. At one point she decided to draw a picture of her current family at the dinner table as a way to show herself that she was able to be a better mother to her children than her own mother had been to her.

Self-Portrait

The client's self-portrait may reveal unconscious thoughts and feelings about herself and her body. Issues such as self-esteem, body image, sexual identity, sexualization, and developmental level may be evident. A small figure in relation to the size of the page may be descriptive of low self-esteem. The degree of sexual differentiation may be related to issues of sexual identity or developmental level. A sexualized looking figure may reflect a tendency toward oversexualization. Missing legs, feet, or hands may reflect feelings of helplessness or passivity. Figure 4, an 18-year-old's self-portrait, suggests the client's oversexualization and helplessness; her dress and body shape are provocative while her hands are behind her back and her feet are missing.

The directions to the self-portrait are:

Draw a picture of yourself.

After Diana finished her self-portrait (Figure 5), I asked her how old her figure looked to her. "Four years old," she replied. Diana was 22. Four was the age at which she had been sexually abused. Diana had unconsciously drawn the figure of a four-year-old; she stated she had not thought before she drew. The information uncovered from the self-portrait helped Diana begin to work on difficulties she was having with her boyfriend — she was literally functioning as a four-year-old when she felt vulnerable with him. In therapy, we simultaneously began to work with the four-year-old while helping the 22-year-old stay in control outside of the sessions.

In working with the self-portrait, the following questions may be used to stimulate discussion with the client:

- What seems interesting or unusual to you?
- How do you look like you feel about yourself?
- What is your mood?
- How do you look like you feel about being a woman?
- How old do you look?
- What is missing and what might that mean?
- What is most prominent and what might that mean?
- What do you like about yourself?
- What do you dislike?

As with the KFD, another way to use the drawing is to ask the client to tell you a story about the person.

Self-portraits drawn at the beginning and end of therapy or

Figure 4 *Self-portrait: Sexualization with missing feet*

Figure 5   *Self-portrait of 22 year old*

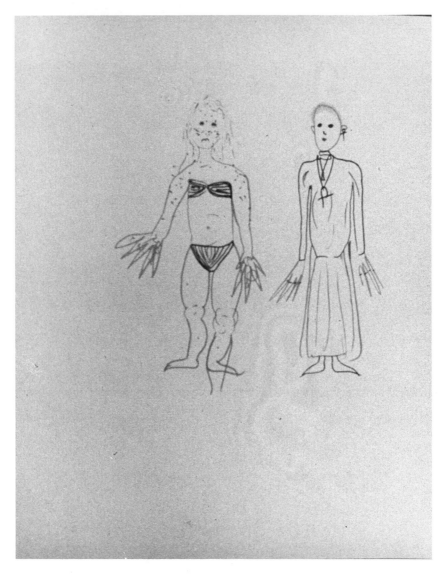

Figure 6,7   *Self-portraits drawn four weeks apart*

Figure 7

with some interval of time between renderings produce visual records of the client's progress (Hammer, 1978). In comparing two self-portraits drawn over time, the client may be asked to consider what is different in the two and what the differences mean in terms of changes she has made or is trying to make.

I have seen self-portraits reflect change even within the brief period of a four-week inpatient hospitalization. For instance, Tamara's self-portrait made at the beginning of her hospitalization (Figure 6) revealed a confused sense of self, which alternated between the exhibitionism of a bikini-clad long-haired figure and the modesty of a nun in short hair. Both figures had long distorted fingers. The bikini-clad figure had dots on her body which Tamara explained showed her sense of feeling "gross, like a freak, like my body is marked." The two figures made in response to the request to draw a picture of herself represented a fairly unusual reaction to the task, leading the treatment team to consider the diagnosis of multiple personality disorder. During a four-week hospitalization, Tamara displayed no other signs or symptoms to support the diagnosis. Just prior to her discharge she repeated the drawing task. Figure 7 demonstrates the integration and increase in functioning that occurred during the hospitalization. In the drawing, Tamara depicts herself in a task-oriented mode with books, as she was returning to college. The dog shows a sense of connection. She has chosen the more protective style of the nun's habit yet has transformed the dress into a stylish outfit topped by a hat. Her hands appear normal. The crescent moon provides a more adaptive context for the black dots as stars rather than symbols of being disfigured.

I have worked with clients who have found the self-portrait particularly enlightening for exploring changes in the sense of self that occur as a result of working through the sexual abuse trauma; a comparison of self-portraits drawn at the beginning of therapy and after the trauma resolution can provide fascinating information about the client's internal shift in self-image.

Aspects of the Drawing

There are several components to drawings that assist the therapist in understanding the client through her artwork. The untrained therapist may start out by simply noticing what is central in the drawing, what is missing, or what is unusual. As with movement, the therapist may observe aspects of the drawing which reflect information the client is unaware of and not ready to integrate. In processing artwork, the therapist may ask the client if she can determine meaning in specific aspects of the drawing. For example, the therapist may ask, "What do you think it means that the door is red?" The therapist's questions will serve as a guide to the client, who will eventually become adept at independently identifying significant art indicators and interpreting her own artwork. The following factors, though not comprehensive, may assist further in deciphering artwork.

Color

> Although "a little knowledge can be a dangerous thing," applying interpretations for the colors we use need not be dangerous if we are objective. Color interpretation needs to consider how the color is used, where it is used on the page, quantity of the color used, what objects or material the color is used on, and the intensity of color displayed. (Furth, 1988, p. 97)

Color has been associated with expression of affect (Birren, 1961; Rorschach, 1942); its intensity may reflect the intensity of affect. The particular meaning of specific colors is widely disputed (Furth, 1988). It is, however, recognized that the meaning of color may be influenced by personal associations and cultural differences (Lusebrink, 1990).

The colors black and red have been found to dominate the artwork of survivors of satanic ritual abuse (Ryder, 1992). "These two colors are most dominant in ritual abuse ceremonies. Black represents the robes. Red represents blood" (p. 55). Objects that are not ordinarily red or black are frequently rendered in those colors.

As will be discussed in more detail below, the use of color may be indicative of defenses. When Eliza drew a picture of herself, she used color in her head and facial features, leaving the body of the figure colorless. This reflected her isolation of affect, her lack of awareness of feelings in the body, and her overintellectualization. Eliza's drawing of anger described in Chapter 1 was executed in strokes of deep red, reflecting the intensity of her angry feeling. Red is often associated with feelings of anger.

Line Quality   Lillian's figure of herself was drawn with faint lines that were barely visible. Such light line pressure may describe hesitancy, restraint, repression, depression, or fearfulness (Hammer, 1958; Machover, 1980); heavy line pressure, on the other hand, may connote assertiveness or inner tension (Hammer, 1958; Ogden, 1977). Line pressure may be so heavy as to cause tearing of the paper. A firm line may signal determination (Buck, 1948; Hammer, 1954). A line appearing to be ruler-straight suggests obsessive-compulsive tendencies (Kaufman & Wohl, 1992), whereas curved lines are consistent with a flexible and healthy personality (Buck, 1948; Hammer, 1954). Lines that are sketchy may describe a lack of confidence or hesitancy (Kaufman & Wohl, 1992). A change in line quality seen in a particular image or part of an image in a drawing may be indicative of conflict. For instance, in Julie's KFD, her brother, who was the perpetrator, was drawn with much greater pressure, producing a thicker line.

Size   Size has been found to correlate with an individual's self-esteem (Hammer, 1978; Ogden, 1977). While a small or tiny drawing may be indicative of feelings of low self-esteem or inferiority, an unusually large image or one that appears to be pressing beyond the boundaries of the page suggests grandiosity, aggression, or a defense against feelings of inadequacy (Hammer, 1964; Kaufman & Wohl, 1992; Ogden, 1977). Figure 8, a self-portrait, shows a tiny figure in the center of the page, descriptive of the artist's low self-esteem. The unusual addition of a second figure in the top left corner suggests identity confusion and raises the possibility of multiplicity.

Details   A picture that appears sparse, empty, or lacking in detail may be reflective of depression or low energy (Hammer, 1958). Too much detail indicates a need to control the environment (Ogden, 1977). While the self-portrait normally does not lend itself to detail beyond the human figure, the KFD and free drawings provide more of an opportunity for the artist to invest the drawing with details. The way that details are arranged on

Figure 8   *Tiny self-portrait*

the page may reflect the artist's inner life. For example, items nonsensically arranged in a drawing may suggest an inner sense of disorganization (Kaufman & Wohl, 1992).

Shading   Shading, most evident in pencil drawings, requires an increased investment in the drawing. Shaded objects or areas are usually associated with conflict and anxiety (Hammer, 1964; Ogden, 1977).

Defenses Seen in Art

The therapist's recognition of defense mechanisms represented in the client's drawings (Levick, 1983) may assist her in supporting the client's defenses rather than prematurely stripping them away, especially in the early stage of therapy. Some of the defenses that the therapist will encounter most frequently with survivors are described below.

Intellectualization   The use of words to keep affects at arms length and to neutralize them is intellectualization, a defense used frequently by survivors. Some of the art shown in this book, especially the collages made with headlines (see Figures 3, 15, and 19), is representative of the defense of intellectualization.

Intellectualization is also seen when an unacceptable idea or feeling is drawn in an elaborate or sophisticated way. Intellectualization is seen in one client's drawing of her anger (Figure 9). She had been terrified of expressing *any* feelings of anger and the drawing gave her a safe, controlled way to approach the emotion.

Regression   Regression may be seen when a drawing appears childlike in relation to other work by the same client or when one element of a drawing is less controlled than the other elements in the same drawing. When regression appears in artwork, we do not always know whether the regression was in response to the topic of the drawing or whether the client regressed for other reasons. With adult survivors, regression is a potential sign of dissociation or the presence of multiple personality disorder (see Chapter 10).

Regression may also appear as a higher level defense when used in the service of the ego (Kris, 1952). For example, a client may

Figure 9   *Intellectualized anger*

deliberately make a painting of childlike finger-painting strokes as an act of creative self-expression.

Denial   Denial may be seen in the absence of fairly obvious details or items. For instance, in a self-portrait, drawing a head alone may reflect denial of the body's existence and feelings of conflict related to the body. In her self-portrait (Figure 10) Cindy drew a feminine looking head but avoided any sexual characteristics in the body by drawing a stick figure. Rebecca, who had a severe eating disorder, drew a self-portrait (Figure 11) without a head. The drawing not only reflects denial of any connection with her body but also shows her distorted body image.

Isolation of Affect   A lack of color may reflect isolation of affect. When one image is colored but another is not, isolation of affect may be operating. A figure or image that presents a separated or unintegrated spot of color on the page suggests isolation of affect.

Art Indicators of Sexual Abuse

Although there is some research investigating art indicators of sexual abuse in children, there is little work with adults. Most recently, research with adults has focused on identifying art indicators of multiple personality disorder, which will be discussed in Chapter 10. Nevertheless, a review of the research and the clinical findings is of interest in identifying potentially significant aspects of artwork. Malchiodi's (1990) caution reflects the difficulty in defining a particular set of art indicators based on the varying impact of trauma, different trauma experiences, and individual differences of victim/survivors, a caution which may apply to the art of adults as well as children:

> Researchers have found commonalities in the art productions of children who have been sexually abused. Although there may be some common graphic indicators in the drawings of children who have been sexually abused, it is difficult to generalize about how this is typified in the art expressions of this population. The images produced will depend on, among other variables, what the child's experience has been and the degree and type of trauma experi-

Figure 10   *Denial: Stick figure*

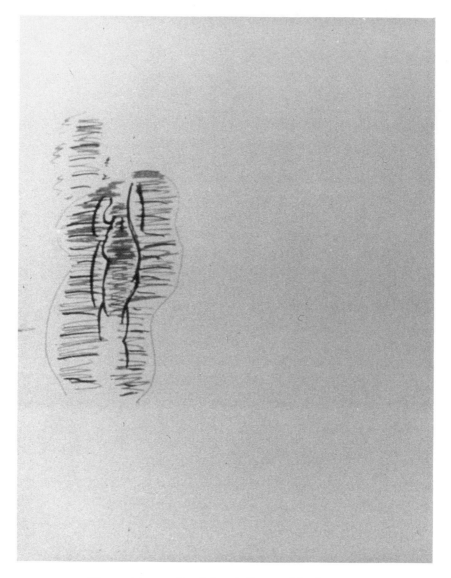

Figure 11   *Denial and distorted body image*

enced. For this reason alone, how the trauma of sexual abuse is expressed visually in the art production cannot be generalized easily or concisely. (p. 143)

The research indicates that there are statistically validated differences in the art of sexually abused subjects but that the findings are not always clinically useful. Kaplan (1991) found that children's KFD drawings showing a family engaged in sexual or intimate activity was a significant indicator of sexual abuse but was present in only 25 percent of sexually abused children's drawings; the absence of such an indicator did not mean the absence of a history of sexual abuse. Although Cohen and Phelps (1985) found significant differences in sexually abused children's drawings, their findings have no clinical utility as the small number of differences in art indicators could be detected only through statistics.

Greenberg (1982) compared Draw-a-Person (DAP) tests for girls who were sexually abused by their fathers with DAPs of nonabused girls. Among the items that were seen significantly more often in drawings of the abused group were: part figures (rather than whole figures), erasures, fragmented lines, and heart-shaped heads. Items found more often in the Kinetic Family Drawings of abused girls were: compartmentalization, heart-shaped figures, lining at the top, and omission of figures. Malchiodi's (1990) clinical findings confirmed the presence of heart-shaped imagery in the art of girls who were father incest victims.

Spring (1986a, 1988) found that the presence of an eye and/or wedge form was a significant indicator of sexual abuse in the artwork of adult women when the symbols were consistently present across a number of drawings.

A study of the Draw-a-Person test by Sidun and Rosenthal (1987) found several statistically significant differences in the artwork of sexually abused and nonabused hospitalized adolescents. A composite of indicators consisting of wedges, circles, and phallic-like objects were drawn significantly more often by the abused group. The single indicator of this composite group that was significant when viewed independently was the enclosed circle. Significance was not found for the wedge form. Hands and fingers were significantly missing in the abused group. Drawings with only heads and no bodies were generally drawn by sexually abused children. Line pressure was significantly heavier in the abused group's drawings.

Jacobson (1993) summarized common symbols in the artwork of traumatized individuals, including: the omission of limbs and mouths related to helplessness and immobilization, missing lower torsos, immobilized bodies, small figures, large red mouths, overpowering tongues, an excess of teeth, facial expressions that do not fit the content depicted, sexual content in the form of trees and monsters, inappropriately sexualized figures, gender confusion, and asexual figures (Galbraith, 1978; Jacobson, 1985; Howard & Jakab, 1969; Kelly, 1984; Spring, 1986; Stember, 1980).

Malchiodi (1990) identified the following additional indicators in the art of sexually abused children: the color red used in a doorway or entrance; encapsulation of a person; disorganization of body parts; artistic regression; and self-deprecation.

Several years ago I suspected that an 18-year-old girl had been sexually abused based on a drawing she produced in my art therapy group (Figure 12). The client had made a serious suicide at-

Figure 12   *Wedge form with enclosed circle*

tempt yet claimed that she had no problems and was feeling fine. The drawing included a wedge shape, an enclosed circle (formed by the thumb and index finger), and phallic-like objects (fingers) found to be statistically significant indicators of sexual abuse in adolescents (Sidun & Rosenthal, 1987). When I asked the client if she had ever been sexually abused, she tearfully revealed that she had been raped a year earlier and she had been afraid to tell anyone; treatment was then able to begin.

Therapists are advised to view the presence of any of the above listed items as a *suggestion* of a history of sexual abuse, to be corroborated by other data, such as clients' self-reports.

5
FLASHBACKS

FLASHBACKS, A SYMPTOM OF post-traumatic stress disorder, are among the most distressing aftereffects of childhood sexual abuse (Briere, 1989; Courtois, 1988; Gil, 1988; Herman & Schatzow, 1987). Unexpectedly intruding upon the survivor, flashbacks can be dangerous when driving, cause embarrassment in social situations, destroy concentration on the job or in school, and ruin sexually intimate moments. Flashbacks can take the form of visual images, physical sensations, auditory images, and strong surges of emotion that are associated with the original trauma.

The relationship of a flashback's content to the original abusive event is not always apparent, forming a sort of sensory puzzle. Typically, a flashback occurs when stimuli in the environment trigger reexperiencing of some aspect of the abuse (Briere, 1989). Although triggers are not always identifiable, there are particular events that are likely to trigger flashbacks. Normative developmental events, including such developmental milestones as a marriage and such developmental crises as the death of a perpetrator, may act as triggers. Flashbacks may be elicited by reminders of the abusive event, whether these are personal experiences, such as a rape or smelling the cologne a perpetrator wore, or bystander experiences, such as watching a television show about childhood abuse. Recovery from substance abuse may remove the dissociative effect of drugs and alcohol that has covered up post-traumatic symptoms, often resulting in an onslaught of flashbacks in the early stages of recovery. Any event related to the abusive experience, such as reporting, remembering, or disclosure may bring on flashbacks. Issues in therapy may also lead to flashbacks, including fear of separation when the therapist is going on vacation, issues around trust, and traumatic transference reactions when the survivor is responding to the therapist as if she were an abuser (Briere & Courtois, 1992).

Flashbacks may yield important information, ultimately assisting the survivor in recollecting traumatic events; yet her first need is to learn to cope with flashbacks, so that she can function on a daily basis without being overwhelmed by anxiety. While flashbacks cannot be stopped, the survivor can learn techniques that will minimize their impact and enable her to regain a sense of control.

A flashback has a powerful pull on the survivor: Suddenly, she is in the past, experiencing abusive events as if they were happening in the present. The survivor needs to fight the pull of the past in order to effectively cope with the flashback. This is not easy, especially when the survivor is feeling fragile, depressed, or exhausted.

Strategies for Coping with Flashbacks

Among the strategies described in the following pages, each individual will find one or more that feel comfortable for her. As treatment progresses, survivors may feel more confident in trying different strategies. For the client in individual therapy, I suggest a strategy based on the client's needs, making modifications in response to her reaction to the exercise. In a group, I present all of the strategies for coping with flashbacks, have clients try them all and then choose which one they would like to use. I then recommend that the strategy be practiced regularly in a non-crisis time.

Grounding Strategies

In order to fight a flashback, the survivor may need to abandon body postures that have habitually served to comfort her. A common self-comforting postural response to a flashback is a variation of the fetal position or a seated posture in which the knees are pulled up to the chest with the head resting on the knees. This posture, which retreats from the present, is based on the survivor's efforts to comfort herself; however, it allows the pull of the past to prevail, preventing the survivor from being grounded in the present, safe reality of adulthood. In other words, the posture that many survivors instinctively maintain during a flashback encourages dissociation, giving the flashback an opening to be the predominant sensory experience. It is not uncommon for survivors habitually to use subtle manifestations of dissociative postures in which legs seldom touch the ground and the upper body is collapsed. Lack of eye contact or lowered gaze can also facilitate dissociation.

It is no easy task for a survivor to trust that the present is safe and to risk taking a posture that allows her to be fully in the here and now. When I run groups for survivors, invariably in the early stages most of the group members sit in dissociative postures and experience postures that would ground them in the present as uncomfortable.

In teaching techniques to cope with flashbacks, I begin by helping clients identify the postures they have previously used to cope with flashbacks. Usually the postures are unconsciously assumed during a flashback unless survivors have already learned coping techniques. The dissociative postures typically employed by survivors in response to flashbacks are also likely to be maintained during stressful episodes. Retreating, dissociative body postures also elicit younger ego states, providing little resistance to retraumatization by flashbacks.

Grounding is a technique that anchors the survivor in the present and minimizes the power of the flashback (Blake-White & Kline, 1985). Kinesthetic, visual, and cognitive grounding strategies can be used in combination or separately. Grounding on a kinesthetic level involves using the body weight actively. A grounding posture involves having both feet on the floor and straightening the spine; there is an active awareness of the body's existence and its connection to the ground in this posture. Legs should be uncrossed, allowing the flow of energy to pass freely through the body. Often when survivors try a grounding posture with both feet on the floor for the first time, they feel exposed or unprotected. For this reason, it is important to present other coping

SEATED GROUNDED POSTURE

1. Ask the client to sit in a posture she typically maintains during a flashback. Discuss this posture (and include eye contact and eye gaze) by posing the following kinds of questions:

   - What are you most aware of when you sit in this position?
   - How old do you feel in the position?
   - Does this posture feel safe? If so, what about the posture feels safe?
   - Are you more aware of your own thoughts and feelings or what is around you when you are in this posture?

   It is important, in discussing grounding, that the client understand that ungrounded postures are protective maneuvers, just as dissociation is a protective maneuver that is no longer working effectively. The client should in no way feel criticized or inadequate for using ungrounded postures.

2. Ask the client to try a grounding posture if the flashback posture she describes is not grounding. If the flashback posture is grounding, reinforce the grounding aspects of the posture. A seated grounding posture consists of legs uncrossed, both feet on the ground, and spine straight. Hands can be on the arms of a chair or resting loosely on the thighs. The client should be directed to feel her feet or shoes making contact with the ground and to notice the back of the thighs and spine making contact with the chair. The head should be erect, with gaze at eye level.

3. Ask the client to experience the grounding posture, especially noticing the feet making contact with the floor and the weight of the body in the chair. Have the client visually note objects around the room. Discuss how comfortable or uncomfortable, safe or unsafe, this posture feels. Suggest that the client become aware of using grounding postures during therapy sessions, at work, or in other activities that require sitting.

   As the therapy progresses, the client may explore any changes in her comfort level with grounding postures.

strategies for the survivor to use when grounded postures feel too threatening.

Chutis (1990) advised stamping the feet so that one is aware that she is able to leave the scene, an option not available in childhood. Stamping the feet not only brings more oxygen into the body, minimizing the effects of dissociation, but also mobilizes the active use of body weight to ground the person in the present. One of my clients, upon experiencing a flashback at home, danced and sang to a particular rock and roll song with a strong beat. The grounding movement of her dancing and the upbeat lyrics successfully distracted her from the flashback material.

Physical contact with an object or a person may also be grounding. One of my clients uses her wedding ring to ground herself,

---

GROUNDING WALK

1. Ask the client to walk around the room and to describe what she is aware of during the walk, both internally and externally. Some clients are so disconnected from themselves that they have little to say in response to this request. If the client feels too self-conscious to try this in a session, ask her to try walking at home, to write down her observations and sensations during the walk, and to bring them into a session.

2. Have the client walk around, noticing how the bottom of each foot makes contact with the ground. Suggest that the client practice walking while noticing how the feet make contact with the ground and how the ground supports the weight of the body.

3. After the client has had some experience with grounded walking, ask her to feel the upright stress of the head, neck, and spine simultaneously while the feet are making contact with the ground.

4. In a flashback, the client can stamp the feet while walking, exaggerating the sensation of contact with the ground, while feeling the upward pull of the head and making eye contact with external objects. The client may practice the stamping, grounded, upright walk.

---

another wears a heavy bracelet, and a third bought a pendant to hang from a keychain that she holds during flashbacks. The therapist can help each survivor choose a grounding strategy that not only feels right for her but is also convenient to her situation. As discussed in Chapter 3, physical touch between therapists and survivors is a sensitive and complex issue. As suggested by Gil (1991), during a particularly bad flashback it is possible for the therapist to offer her hand in such a way as to give the client the option of accepting or rejecting the offer. The therapist may be faced with a client who appears so drawn into a flashback and in such a deeply dissociated state that she is unresponsive to any verbal interventions. While it may be tempting to touch clients in these situations, I have found that they may experience any touch as part of the flashback, so out of contact with the present are they at those times. It is recommended that after the first such episode of nonresponsive, deep dissociation, the therapist and client develop an agreement as to how the therapist is to intervene. Often clients can tell us exactly what will be helpful to them.

Visual grounding strategies include making eye contact, visually scanning the current environment in order to orient to the present, and developing visual grounding devices. Visual grounding devices can be photographs or imaginary visual images. One of my clients who was having difficulty with flashbacks at work used photographs of her children on her desk to visually ground herself. Another client was able to summon the visual image of her safe place (described in Chapter 6) during flashbacks. Yet another client drew a picture representing feelings of safety which she kept on her bedside table. This is an example of using the skill of dissociation as a positive, voluntary coping strategy; the survivor can imagine that she is someplace else other than the present. It is highly recommended that the client who has generally kept her eyes closed during flashbacks try to keep them open to help ground herself. However, even with eyes open some survivors continue to see images that are part of the flashback. For these clients, the physical grounding strategies are more helpful.

Some survivors actually induce a dissociative state by staring at an object; this may be done in a somewhat unconscious way. For these survivors, visual grounding should include shifting of eye gaze from one object to another.

Directing the gaze at eye level rather than downward is also helpful. One of my clients habitually looked down during flashbacks. At one point in a group, while she was having a flashback, I asked her to describe what she saw. She described seeing large shoes (the group members' shoes), which reminded her of being a small and helpless child. After the flashback ended, we discussed eye gaze during flashbacks; once she realized the regressive effect of her downward gaze, she was much more willing to try to look straight ahead rather than down.

Cognitive grounding involves saying reassuring thoughts to oneself in the midst of a flashback, such as, "This is just in your mind. You are an adult now and you are safe." Clients may choose to write grounding, reassuring statements on index cards to be carried in a pocket or wallet so that they are handy during a flashback. Some survivors with multiple personality disorder have found cognitive strategies the most helpful. Due to her extreme disconnection from the body, the MPD client has great difficulty physically grounding herself or staying present visually during flashbacks. The statements invoked through a cognitive strategy appear to be more likely to be heard by many personalities; one personality may be designated to make comforting statements to child personalities or to all the personalities. For more coping strategies especially designed for multiples, see *Getting Through the Day* by Nancy Napier.

The ultimate goal of a flashback strategy is to connect the body and the mind, anchoring the survivor in the here and now. Deep breathing connects body and mind in the present through a combination of kinesthetic, visual, and cognitive grounding. It may also be undertaken in just about any situation and is particularly useful in public places, allowing the survivor to handle the flashback without calling attention to herself. Deep breathing can also be effective for the survivor who needs the protection of a retreating, dissociative posture and feels unsafe assuming a grounded posture.

Realistic expectations about flashback strategies will help survivors feel a greater sense of mastery. Therapists should educate clients that flashbacks cannot be stopped but that their effects can be contained. If a client expects that flashbacks will no longer be upsetting once she uses a flashback strategy, she may feel frus-

FLASHCARD

1. Ask the client to come up with several grounding statements that assure her that she is only experiencing a flashback, that the flashback is not really happening, and that she is safe now. It is important that the statements come from the client.

2. The grounding statements can be written on an index card or a piece of paper to create a "flashcard." Determine what locations (such as the bathroom or her desk) are most problematic for the survivor in terms of containing flashbacks. Decide on the size of the paper for the statements: if the client wants to carry the statements in a wallet, an index card or small piece of paper is appropriate; if the client wants to have the statements clearly visible by posting them on a wall or a bulletin board, a larger piece of paper will be needed.

3. Decide if the survivor's or the therapist's handwriting will be most effective. The therapist's handwriting can act as a transitional object for a client who does not yet have much ego strength. If the client is experiencing some negative transferential feelings, her own handwriting will be most effective. I usually ask the client if she wants to write her statement or if she wants me to write it. In the later stages of treatment, the client should be encouraged to rely on her own handwriting.

4. For writing statements, have the survivor choose a colored marker that represents safety, reassurance, or strength.

5. The grounding statements are written with the colored marker on the flashcard. Other directions for coping with flashbacks that the survivor has determined are effective can be added. Use the exercises in the other boxes to help the survivor come up with one or more flashback strategies if comforting words are insufficient.

6. Once the client uses it, review the strategy and decide if any changes should be made in the flashcard so that the most effective strategies can be captured in writing.

GROUNDING THROUGH BREATHING

The advantage of grounding through breathing is that it can be used at any time and any place. Its subtlety allows it to be used in public places.

1. Teach the client to breath diaphragmatically, so that the diaphragm expands on the inhale. The diaphragm can be located by placing the hand on the abdominal area and feeling the stomach expand outward on the inhale.

    Therapist: "Breath evenly and calmly, feeling the diaphragm expand with oxygen on the inhale and feeling it deflate on the exhale. All of your attention is focused on expanding and contracting the diaphragm with each breath."

2. Therapist: "Each exhale is accompanied by saying a number to yourself. Count ten exhales. If you still need help calming yourself after ten breaths, continue to count in groups of ten until you feel ready to stop."

3. After the client tries counting, she can try saying a calming statement to herself on the inhale. She should choose a calming statement that feels right to her. Examples of calming statements are:

    *   "I am breathing in calm air."
    *   "I am safe."
    *   "In comes the calm air."

    Another variation is to add a statement to be said during the exhale. Example: "I am inhaling calm air; I am exhaling anxiety."

NOTE: Clients who experience anxiety as a result of heightened awareness in the throat, chest, or abdominal area during deep breathing may find relief by focusing on the sensation of the breath against the nostrils, a classic meditation technique.

trated or feel like a failure if she continues to be distressed by them. Many survivors find it helpful to know that they can do something during a flashback rather than be fully absorbed by the past. It is important for survivors not only to discover strategies that fit their individual needs but also to realize that the techniques become easier to use over time.

It is also reassuring to survivors to know that they do not have to process every flashback. Many survivors find it helpful to relate the details of a flashback after it occurs. However, discussing the ramifications of the material may be overwhelming. The survivor can create a special storage strategy to contain the impact of the material until she is ready to deal with it in therapy (see Chapter 7). Alternately, the survivor can work with the flashback material to create a more nurturing outcome, if she is not ready to do memory work or if she is in the midst of memory work but needs help containing her anxiety. For instance, Lillian had a recurrent flashback of looking down on herself and seeing her hands tied over her head as they were when she was raped at the age of five. In order to calm herself from this upsetting image, she imagined untying her hands and rubbing soothing lotion on her hands and wrists. She was also able to use this "undoing" technique with nightmares and bad dreams. It should be noted that Lillian was unable to use this strategy until her second go-round in therapy. In order to use these techniques outside the therapy sessions, the

---

FIGHTING A FLASHBACK

1. Have the client use the seated or walking grounded posture described above. Have her identify an object in the room to visually ground herself through eye contact.

2. Have the client stamp her feet and do deep breathing, counting exhales while maintaining visual contact with the chosen object.

3. Have the client evaluate which strategies she was able to maintain and which she may have unknowingly discontinued. Also, discuss which strategy was most effective. The client may decide to stick with one of the grounding strategies rather than using many at once.

client needs not only to have attained object constancy but also to believe that she is entitled to feel better.

Flashbacks can provide valuable pieces of the survivor's memory. In Chapter 11 I present strategies that use flashback imagery to facilitate memory retrieval. Some clients need to record the flashback material either through writing or artmaking as a means of catharsis. Frequently the client is not ready to do any further work on the traumatic material once the flashback is committed to paper. If the process of writing or drawing the flashback does not appear to trigger increased flooding, this particular technique is probably effective for the survivor; the writings or drawings may be stored until the survivor is ready to do further processing.

Relaxation Skills

Relaxation skills can help the survivor establish a greater sense of control as well as recreate a more positive relationship with the body. Relaxation exercises can help with anxiety, sleep problems, intrusive thoughts, and somatic complaints, in addition to flashbacks. Relaxation skills can also address the anxiety that the survivor experiences after the flashback is over when recapitulating the content or affect associated with the flashback. Through relaxation exercises the survivor may recapture a more comforting kinesthetic state, which may counter the distressing physical sensations experienced through body memories or kinesthetic flashbacks.

Because many survivors have had few opportunities to learn self-soothing skills, learning relaxation exercises can be viewed as a developmental task that enhances the survivor's self-concept as an adult. The therapist may take on the role of educator to the client, teaching self-soothing strategies, explaining what is "normal," and providing an atmosphere of acceptance that allows the survivor to reveal feelings of anxiety and neediness.

Relaxation exercises, in order to be effective, must address the multidimensional nature of the survivor's anxiety. Typically, there are three modes in which tension or anxiety is manifested: (1) kinesthetically in the form of somatic sensations; (2) visually in the form of mental imagery; and (3) cognitively in the form of distressing thoughts. A kinesthetic manifestation may take the form of feeling unable to breathe or to stop shaking. Visual mani-

RELAXATION THROUGH TENSION*

This classic exercise is based on the premise of increasing tension to create relaxation. Each tightening of muscles should be held for five seconds. The client may choose to count while holding the tension. It may be helpful when doing the exercise for the first time for the client to pay attention to the contrast of the sensations in the muscles during tensing and immediately thereafter. The sensation of the muscles after the tensing or tightening may be the client's first conscious awareness of the sensation of relaxation. Some clients may have difficulty with certain body parts; in such cases, such areas may be eliminated from the exercise.

This exercise can be tried first in the office with the therapist reading the directions. The client may then practice on her own by reading the directions or following a cassette tape of the therapist reading the directions. It is recommended that the exercise initially be done while the client is sitting in a chair; she may choose to do the exercise while lying down once she has some practice with it.

Directions for Relaxation

1. Using the dominant hand, make a tight fist. (*Hold for five seconds and then release. This direction follows each step.*)
2. Using the dominant biceps, push the elbow down against the arm of the chair.
3. Using the nondominant hand, make a tight fist.
4. Using the nondominant biceps, push the elbow down against the arm of the chair.
5. Lift the eyebrows.
6. Squint the eyes and wrinkle the nose.
7. Bite down and pull the corners of the mouth down.
8. Pull the chin downward without touching the chest.
9. Take a deep breath and pull the shoulder blades back.
10. Pull in the stomach.
11. Push the back of the dominant thigh into the seat of the chair.
12. Flex the dominant foot, pointing the toe toward the head.
13. Turn the dominant foot inward while pointing and curling the toes.
14. Push the back of the nondominant thigh into the seat of the chair.
15. Flex the nondominant foot, pointing the toe toward the head.
16. Turn the nondominant foot inward, while pointing and curling the toes.

*Based on Bernstein and Borkevec's (1973) 16 muscle groups.

festations may involve seeing colors, images and abstract shapes, such as one client's description: "everything feels black and swirling around me." Cognitive manifestations are negative and distorted thoughts, such as, "I can't handle this" or "Something terrible is going to happen to me."

Each individual may experience anxiety in any combination of the three modes at any given time. For example, when Betsy became anxious at work she began to have difficulty breathing, would imagine that a hand was grabbing her throat, and would think, "I am going to die." Sometimes she would only have trouble with her breathing. Eventually, in therapy Betsy was ready to explore the source of this anxiety reaction, connecting it to her childhood abuse. However, during the early phase of therapy Betsy's greatest need was to function at work. Relaxation skills provided a means of relief without jeopardizing her ego functioning.

For the survivor who is experiencing frequent flashbacks, relaxation exercises usually need to be quite active, encompassing kinesthetic activity such as deep breathing or active tensing of muscles, rather than simply relying on imagery or cognition. The survivor will need to be actively engaged in the exercise so as not to be receptive to the sensory intrusions of flashbacks. A thorough investigation of the manifestations of the client's anxiety will provide the information needed to formulate a relaxation exercise. The client should be given the opportunity to try the relaxation exercise and describe her experience using the exercise.

A relaxation exercise can be introduced at a time when the client is reporting extreme anxiety outside of the therapy sessions. However, it is important for both therapist and client to recognize the difficulty that the client may have in trying something new in the midst of a stressful situation. For the survivor with an extremely chaotic life, the concentration required to undertake a relaxation exercise is often not available. Sometimes a cassette recording of a relaxation exercise provides enough structure to support the client who would be unable to try the exercise on her own. The client may buy commercially-made tapes or the therapist can make a tape of the relaxation exercise. As therapy progresses, many clients who were unsuccessful earlier in the therapy gain the ability to use relaxation.

6
SAFETY

TYPICALLY, VICTIMS OF TRAUMA experience a loss of basic trust in the goodness and security of their world (Herman, 1992; Janoff-Bulman, 1992). For the sexual abuse survivor, the betrayal of trust inflicted by the abuser often generalizes to an impending sense of disaster and the constant possibility of betrayal. As a violation of the child's body and ego boundaries, sexual abuse strips the child of her sense of separateness and leads to a chronic feeling of being unsafe. Because the loss of boundaries is associated with the abused child's experiences of pain or betrayal, intimacy may be fraught with conflict for the adult survivor.

The Impact of a Lack of Safety

Entering therapy presents the survivor with many paradoxes around safety. Although there may be some relief at having made the decision to seek treatment, there may be fear of closeness and dependency along with fear of exploring the past. The therapist needs to be sensitive to the client's vulnerability, which often appears as resistance. The client's lack of trust and concern with safety may result in her being avoidant, guarded, or oppositional. For this reason, the request to try using art or body-centered interventions in the first few sessions may be threatening for some clients. However, the client may well be more open as the therapy progresses. In addition, some clients have difficulty successfully trying any interventions outside the therapy sessions at this point in the therapy, due to their lack of trust in the therapist and/or their problems concentrating or organizing themselves.

While issues around safety may manifest themselves in subtle ways in the course of therapy, the beginning of treatment may include an evaluation of the extent to which lack of feeling safe has influenced the survivor's lifestyle choices. Activities related to sleeping, using the bathroom, socializing, being alone, and traveling are prone to difficulty. Among the kinds of restrictions feeling unsafe has produced in my clients are: sleeping in clothing, seldom taking baths, refraining from social contact, avoiding being alone, and refusing to travel at night. Sometimes the avoidance of certain activities becomes so habitual and secretive that the survivor believes her actions are normal. Discussing safety in therapy, identifying what feels unsafe and what measures the survivor has taken to feel safer, brings the issue of safety into conscious awareness. Such a discussion may elicit feelings of guilt and shame in the client; the therapist needs to help her accept that her safety strategies, no matter how silly or restrictive, are a normal and understandable response to trauma. The survivor's task, at this point, is to begin to identify how and to what extent she is still reacting to the events of the past and disregarding the reality of the present.

While many survivors have a good awareness of situations that feel unsafe, there is often little awareness of situations that provide a greater sense of safety. Many survivors unconsciously utilize coping strategies to increase safety, for instance, wearing neutral-colored or shapeless clothing, sleeping with the light on, and keeping the television on when alone. The therapist can help the client identify safety strategies and reframe them so that she feels she is taking control over her anxiety. The identification of safety strategies provides a key to accessing feelings of calmness, which may then be generalized to other situations. The therapist is more likely to have success in identifying safety strategies if the client is asked, "What helps you feel *safer*?" or "What helps you feel a little less scared?" rather than, "What helps you feel *safe*?" Many survivors never feel safe. Raising the possibility that there are times when the survivor feels slightly less threatened will increase her hopefulness. While truly gaining a sense of safety is often a long-term endeavor for survivors of severe sexual abuse, early on they can learn some strategies that elicit a greater sense of calmness. Issues of safety will be explored continuously during the early stages of therapy. As Herman (1992) explains, the survivor must develop the ability to feel safe from the self as well as in the environment.

When safety is the object of discussion in therapy, the client may benefit from making a drawing or collage that represents the issue for her, reflecting fears as well as strengths. Figure 13 shows Sandra's struggle with feeling safe. Her art helped her hold onto the reality of her situation, rather than being swept away by her fears and fantasies.

Boundaries

Relationships in the survivor's life, including the therapy relationship, may elicit problems with boundaries. She may be distant with others, she may be overidentified with others, or she may

---

IMAGINING SAFETY

1. Ask the client to draw a picture of herself showing to what degree she feels safe in the world.

2. Discuss the picture with the client, asking her to tell as much about the picture as possible.

3. Ask the client to draw another picture showing what she would look like if she felt safe or what would cause her to feel safe. Explain that she can put anything she wants in her picture because this is a creative exercise. She may need the therapist's help in coming up with a picture showing that she feels safe.

4. Discuss the picture with the client. Although a picture may be highly imaginative, there may be some grain of reality in it that gives cues as to what the client can do to feel safer, either figuratively or literally. For instance, a drawing that showed a client isolated from people led to her decision to try to stay away from her current friends and think about making new friends who were more supportive to her. Another client drew a picture of a door with large locks on it. Discussion revealed that the client would feel safer if she had a lock put on her bedroom door; she actually did this and felt slightly safer.

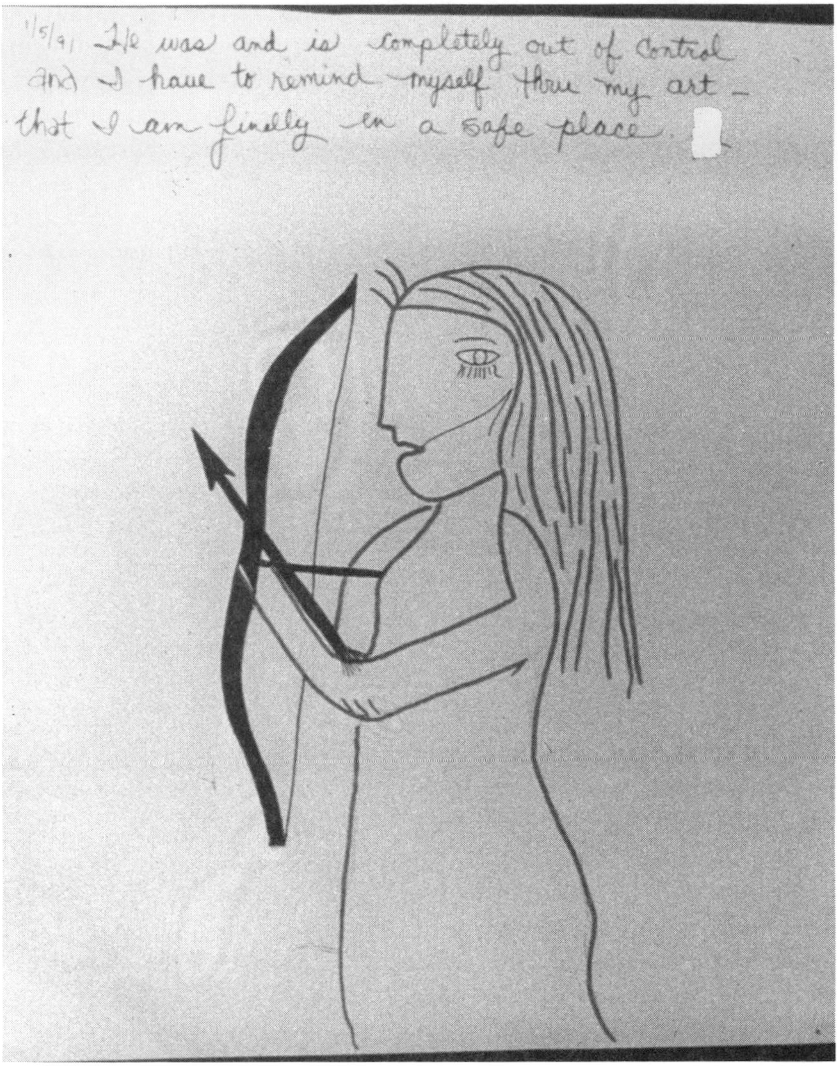

Figure 13   *Art as a means for feeling safety*

fluctuate between the two. Her sense of separateness may be too permeable or too rigid. She may lose her ability to set limits with friends and family. I was reminded of this issue when a client came for her second therapy appointment accompanied by a male neighbor she had befriended just the week before. She wanted him to sit in on the session because, "I've been telling him everything and this way I won't have to repeat everything to him after I see you—he'll be able to hear for himself." The client's boundaries were so loose that she was unable to differentiate the private matters of therapy from conversation with a relative stranger. The loss of boundaries reflects the destruction of the sense of self that sexual abuse imposes on the child.

In therapy the survivor can explore the issue of boundaries. Felice, who was having difficulty feeling a solid sense of separate-

---

IMAGINARY BUBBLE

1. The client is going to create an imaginary protective bubble as a means of exploring boundaries and safety. Have her determine how far away from her body she wants to place the protective bubble. The distance around the body is called the kinesphere. When the arms are fully extended, the area defined is called far kinesphere. Middle kinesphere is located halfway between far kinesphere and the body. Near kinesphere is the area closest to the body. Some clients may want the bubble to be beyond far kinesphere.

2. When the distance from the body of the bubble has been established, have the client define and then explore with her hands the full extent of the walls of the bubble, from top to bottom and side to side. To make the bubble feel more real, the therapist may ask the client the following questions:

   • What do the walls of the bubble feel like?
   • Are they clear or colored?
   • How strong are they?
   • How would you like to feel inside the bubble?
   • What would it be like to have a bubble between you and other people?

3. If the client feels comfortable in the therapist's office, she may stand up and walk around the room with the bubble surrounding her. A processing discussion should follow. Discuss with the client any insights which she has had as a result of experiencing the bubble.

---

ness and safety, created an imaginary protective barrier between herself and other people. By imagining a protective bubble around herself, she kinesthetically experienced a feeling of distance and separation from those around her. The bubble linked the issues of safety and boundaries. When she was in a group of people, a situation which generally elicited fear and anxiety, she tried to recall the feeling of the bubble's protection. Felice agreed to use the exercise outside of therapy only after she had determined that there were no external indicators of danger, so that she did not block out real signs of danger. Trained as an artist, Felice was a highly visual person who envisioned her protective barrier as the color pink. At times when she felt especially in need of protection, she wore pink clothing. She made a drawing of her protective barrier (Figure 14), which showed her need to feel that *no one* could touch her. Much later in her therapy she was able to have a more moderate attitude about touch, losing her all-or-nothing thinking about the issue.

Figure 14   *Protective barrier*

Another exercise concerning safety commonly used by therapists working with survivors is "creating a safe place." The survivor imagines a safe place, either real or imaginary, embellishing the image with all aspects of sensory experience: visual, kinesthetic, auditory, olfactory, and sometimes gustatory. A common scene is the beach; the survivor would, for example, imagine the color of the sky, the feeling of the sun on her skin, the sound of the waves crashing on the shore, the smell of the ocean, and the taste of salt on her lips. A similar exercise describes a "power

---

CREATING A SAFE PLACE

1. Ask the client to imagine a safe place. It can be an imaginary place or a place that she has been to before.

2. Have the client experience all senses in the safe place:

   • Describe what you see, paying special attention to colors.
   • What sounds do you hear?
   • What posture is your body in?
   • How does the air feel against your skin?
   • How do you feel?
   • What fragrances do you smell?
   • Notice your breathing.

   If appropriate, ask the client if she notices any taste on her lips or in her mouth.

3. Have the client choose a souvenir that will remind her of the safe place. The souvenir can be a color, a symbol, a song. The client may choose to use the souvenir to remind her of feeling safe; she may actually make a collage of it, purchase it, or somehow make it part of her daily life.

4. The client may make a collage or a drawing that represents the safe place. The drawing or collage can be used to elicit feelings of safety at any time.

5. Have the client decide on a location to keep the drawing or collage as a visual reminder of feeling safe.

---

place," a location where the survivor feels strong and powerful. A good homework assignment is for the survivor to make a drawing or collage of her safe place or power place, which will support her eliciting the feelings related to the place when she is away from the therapist. As a further aid to accessing the desired feelings of safety or strength, the survivor may listen to a cassette of evocative music or natural sounds (such as the ocean) while reviewing all of the sensory cues that relate to the place.

7
COPING MECHANISMS

IN PREPARATION FOR THE arduous work of resolving the abuse, the survivor is advised to have a well developed repertoire of coping mechanisms. These can assist with the flooding of affect and exacerbation of symptoms that commonly accompany such work. For many survivors the development of coping skills is essential early in treatment, since they come into therapy feeling flooded or overwhelmed. Coping mechanisms, therefore, are of immediate benefit to many clients. It is not unusual to spend several sessions with clients simply strategizing how they might cope with the intensity of their feelings once they leave the therapist's office.

It is important for the therapist to distinguish when the client is truly in need of a coping strategy and when she needs the therapist to be empathically present while she abreacts. The intensity of the grief and rage experienced by many survivors may be searingly painful for the therapist to tolerate; yet the expression of such intense affect may be necessary for resolution of the sexual abuse trauma. The client herself needs to learn how to tolerate such affect before she can benefit from its expression; initially, at least, she will need the therapist's help.

Often events in the client's history indicate the need for coping skills. These include recent psychiatric hospitalization, self-destructive behaviors, or poor daily functioning. Educating the client about the need to possess coping skills before exploring traumatic material allows her to assume a collaborative role in determining the course of treatment.

For the therapist new to work with trauma survivors, the idea of helping the client stop the flow of affect in a therapy session may be new. Many of us have been trained to encourage the expression of feelings in therapy. However, the flooding of intense emotion that often accompanies traumatic memories supports a greater sense of caution where expression of affect is concerned.

In this chapter, I describe two basic kinds of coping strategies. The first serves to contain the flow of feelings and thoughts, preventing the client from becoming overwhelmed and/or constantly flooded. The second provides an outlet for intense affect, one that is healthier than the dysfunctional coping strategies the client has habitually used. Regardless of the type of strategy chosen, it is crucial that the therapist convey to the client that she has been coping to the best of her abilities. The therapist's suggestion of alternative coping mechanisms must in no way be seen as criticism of the client.

Creating an Image for the Process of Healing

In the early phase of therapy the therapist can serve as an educator, teaching the client what to expect from the process of healing from sexual abuse. There are several metaphors for healing which I describe to clients; then I may ask the client to develop her own image, story, or metaphor representing her healing journey (Combs

---

CREATING A METAPHOR FOR HEALING

Some clients already have their own metaphor or image for healing from sexual abuse implanted in their minds, although it may be unconscious or barely conscious. Some clients will be able to create their own metaphor, either without much prompting from the therapist or with the help of hearing about other metaphors. Other clients will identify with an already existing metaphor. After the client clarifies the metaphor with which she identifies, have her make a collage or drawing representing the metaphor. She may want to hang it up at home in a visible spot.

& Freedman, 1990; Dolan, 1991). The metaphor allows the survivor to see the paradoxical and multidimensional nature of healing: that some amount of pain will be experienced in order to resolve the sexual abuse trauma; that healing is episodic or cyclical. A healing metaphor provides a point of reference when the going gets rough, while offering the hope of a positive outcome.

One client used the metaphor of a tunnel. At first, when she began to work on sexual abuse in therapy, she could see the light at the entrance of the tunnel from which she had come. As time went on and she moved into the middle of the tunnel, she could no longer see the light where she had come in and she could not see any light at the end of the tunnel. In darkness, she felt hopeless, feeling that she would be lost in the dark forever. It helped her to remember that she was in the middle of the tunnel and that the light at the end of the tunnel existed, even though she could not see it yet. The client drew a picture of the rays of light at the end of the tunnel, an image that represented hope in the midst of the darkness.

Another client developed her healing metaphor around the movie *Aliens II*. The gist of her metaphor was that she was forced to become a fighter to save her little-girl-self from alien monsters, which represented her abuse. With my encouragement, she developed a kinesthetic image of the fighter; this allowed her to experience herself as strong and powerful in her body.

The concept of developing strength to become a fighter or have a fighting spirit may represent a perceptual shift for some survivors; yet it is necessary for the survivor who sees herself as helpless. Although the survivor may feel in no way like a fighter, the ability to create such images of herself will give her some positive self-images to emulate and reinforce. The idea of having strength or being a fighter may be overwhelming, but introducing the idea of *training* to be stronger may help the survivor acquire an expectation of incremental growth. Because many survivors experience all-or-nothing thinking (i.e., I'm not strong now and I will never be), I sometimes introduce the idea of incremental change by telling a story about a friend who decided she wanted to run in a marathon even though she had never run more than a city block. John Briere (1989) has described a similar metaphor. I describe how my friend spent two years training for the race, slowly building her strength and endurance, sometimes not even realizing that she was making progress because each gain was so small. I then ask the client to develop an image of herself as a fighter or "Woman Warrior." Both visual and kinesthetic images can anchor the concept of the survivor as a fighter. As a homework assignment, the client may create a collage or drawing of her fighting side or strong part, which will reinforce more positive self-concepts.

Figure 15 shows Joan's "Woman Warrior" collage. It was notable that two years earlier Joan had made a drawing with a similar theme and immediately after had made a drawing showing herself cutting her arm. At the time she had been unable to maintain the

---

THE WOMAN WARRIOR

1. Have the client imagine herself as strong or as a "Woman Warrior." The therapist may explain to the client that she does not need to actually feel this way—she need only imagine what it would be like to feel this way. She may think of a female figure, either real or fictional, who appears strong and imagine what it would be like to feel like her or inhabit her body.

2. Have the client describe how she feels as a "Woman Warrior." The therapist may clarify and reflect the client's verbalizations, as well as ask the client questions which will elicit kinesthetic sensations of strength, such as:

   • What posture are you in as a "Woman Warrior"?
   • How and where do you feel a sense of strength in your body?

3. The therapist then describes the postures and sensations of the "Woman Warrior" while the client focuses on the accompanying sensations and feelings.

4. The client should have created a body posture along with adjectives that describe internal bodily sensations, thoughts, and feelings. She may be reminded to practice the "Woman Warrior" and pretend she is her when feeling the need to be stronger.

5. The client may make a collage or drawing of the "Woman Warrior."

Figure 15   *"The Woman Warrior"*

image of herself as a warrior and had clearly given me the message that she was not ready to be strong. Two years later, she made the collage at my suggestion. The piece took several days, as she had to look for headlines and images in magazines, cut them out, and arrange them on the page. She had internalized a more enduring sense of strength during the subsequent two years. As can be seen from the small headline, "the fine art of faking it," Joan still has difficulty feeling powerful. However, at times "faking it" may give the survivor a way to begin to experience herself differently as a prelude to actually feeling the new sense of self as real.

Collage is a powerful art tool that is especially appropriate for clients who do not like drawing or are uncomfortable with their artistic abilities. One of my clients who perfectionistically obsessed about her drawing skills found collage to be much less anxiety provoking. While the finished collage represents a highly expressive product, the tasks of finding images, cutting them out, organizing them on a page, and gluing them are extremely containing. The tools required for collage are magazines, a glue stick (but any form of glue will work), and scissors (presenting contraindications for the seriously self-injurious or suicidal client). "Like drawings, collages allow material to be expressed in a way that can't be done through words alone, though words themselves are often an important part of collages" (Cohen, 1992, p. 14). One of my clients was able to make collages about her thoughts and feelings concerning her sexual abuse, which she was too afraid to verbalize in therapy. The collage gave her a way to deal with overwhelming material without having to talk about it before she was ready.

Titrating the Process

While at her job as an editor, Irene found herself frequently in tears and unable to concentrate due to constantly thinking about our therapy sessions. In therapy she cried often and had great difficulty pulling herself together by the end of each session. Irene explained that she had been repressing all her feelings for years and that once she entered therapy she felt as if a dam had burst, causing the many years of feelings to come pouring out. Irene's experience is not atypical; many survivors go from numbness to flooding. Clearly, expression of affect was giving Irene no sense of relief and containment was indicated. Irene agreed with me that she needed help containing her emotions while still having access to them in smaller doses.

Containment enables the client to use her dissociative abilities in a positive, empowering way. In Irene's case, she consciously made a choice to keep certain thoughts and feelings out of consciousness. Although it often takes practice for the client to use dissociation and compartmentalization as containment, some clients can do this with surprising ease. Although sometimes this is a long-term endeavor, my experience has given me an enormous sense of optimism about survivors' abilities to develop the capacity to contain thoughts and feelings outside of therapy. I know of several clients who initially appeared too fragile to succeed at containment, but after five to seven years of therapy, including several hospitalizations, they began to successfully use containment strategies outside of therapy sessions, allowing them to function much better on a day-to-day basis. Higher-functioning survivors may be able to use containment almost immediately. Because containment requires certain dissociative abilities, I have found that for survivors who are recovering from substance abuse, containment strategies may not come easily; having relied on drugs or alcohol as the catalyst for dissociation, the recovering survivor may have fewer resources with which to distance herself from feelings or memories.

In Irene's case, I asked her to come up with an image that represented a good storage place for her feelings while allowing her to retrieve a little bit of them. She decided that her feelings could be stored in my desk drawer. I then asked her to think of what she could do when she was at work and she began to feel overwhelmed by her feelings. She decided that she would imagine placing them in an envelope, seal the envelope, and place it in her purse, so that the feelings would be available during a therapy session if she needed them.

It was a novel idea to Irene that thinking about her abuse could be contained to the therapy sessions. During the first two months after we came up with the strategy, Irene continued to have difficulty at work but was able to use the containment strategy in the therapy sessions. Initially, I had given her the responsibility of keeping track of the time in the session so as to start putting her emotions into my desk drawer ten minutes before the session was to end. However, Irene soon let me know that she wanted me to be the timekeeper, telling her when it was time to put her feelings away. After several months Irene no longer needed me to help her contain her feelings and was able to successfully contain them in and out of therapy.

The client can create her own image or strategy for titrating affects and memories. One of my clients, who would go through phases of having frequent flashbacks and nightmares, found an old jewelry box at a flea market, which she decorated with magazine pictures of weightlifters, symbolizing her strength in being able to survive and her determination to continue surviving. When she had a flashback, she jotted down its content on a piece of

CREATING A CONTAINER

1. Have the client imagine an object or a place where her thoughts, feelings, memories, or flashbacks can be stored. The client does not necessarily have to feel this will work at this stage.

2. The client can find an actual object for storage, such as a small file box, or she can draw a picture of her container. Containers can be decorated with paint, drawings, or collage. For the client who needs the concrete experience of writing down thoughts, feelings, etc., on a piece of paper and depositing it somewhere, an actual container is helpful, especially one with a small lock. If the client chooses a real container, discuss together where the container will be kept. Some clients need to keep the container out of sight to minimize being stimulated by memories or feelings, while others need the container in a visible location as a reminder to use it.

3. The client may wish to retrieve memories or flashbacks from the container when she feels ready to handle the feelings associated with them.

paper, folded it up, and placed it in the box. This strategy helped her put the frightening images out of her mind until she felt ready to focus on them, either on her own or in her therapy sessions.

Another client felt "dirty" from the images of her flashbacks and the intense feelings elicited. She used deep breathing, imagining that she was exhaling what she called "black goop," which represented the feelings and images related to the flashbacks; she then imagined that she inhaled blue "healing, healthy air." Another containing technique, typically used in hypnosis, is to have the patient imagine that memories are viewed on a movie or television screen. It is not necessary for the patient to be in trance to use this technique, as the dissociative patient frequently has the capacity to use such strategies effectively without a formal hypnotic induction. One of my clients found it helpful to draw a picture of a movie screen designed in an art deco style to differentiate it from any movie screen that she was likely to actually encounter. She drew the picture wallet-sized and carried it with her to assist in coping with memories. Joan Turkus (1990) has described using an image of a video cassette storage box to help contain a client who was constantly abreacting; the client's memories were seen as video cassettes that could be stored away in the box.

Reinforcing Nonregressive Body Postures

The client's interest in containment provides the therapist with an opportunity to give feedback about body postures and nonverbal behavior. If the therapist carefully observes the client in sessions, she will probably find that the client's nonverbal behavior changes markedly when she is overwhelmed or flooded. Some behaviors that the client may exhibit are: eyes closed, rocking, repetitive gestures or movements, lack of groundedness, rapid or shallow breathing, and collapsed upper torso. When asked how old they feel in the midst of being flooded or overwhelmed, clients frequently answer that they feel like a child or a little girl.

The client may show very different nonverbal behavior when she is feeling more in control. Typically, the client who feels relatively in control will exhibit good eye contact, spontaneous gesturing, groundedness, even breathing, and an upward postural stress in the lower body. The client can begin to build awareness of her "in control" nonverbal behavior. She may give the "in control" ego state an appropriately descriptive name to serve as a cue to anchor the posture. Some clients may spontaneously describe this as their adult part. The part may also represent the survivor's "internal protector" (Calof, 1992; Harkaway, 1991; Krieger, 1991), although internal protectors are sometimes child parts who may undertake more regressive postures; the goal at this point is to reinforce a body state that is not regressive. Although the client may initially need the therapist to remind her to use the "adult" nonverbal behavior when she is feeling overwhelmed, eventually she will be able to do this on her own.

When a client with limited coping skills becomes flooded in a therapy session, it can be effective for the therapist to tell the client to sit up straight, look at the therapist, and take a deep breath. It seems to refocus the client if she changes her posture, moves to a different seat, or gets up and stretches or paces briefly. As in the case of a client experiencing flashbacks, the flooded or overwhelmed client may benefit from grounding strategies.

ANCHORING "IN CONTROL" OR "ADULT" POSTURES

1. Both the therapist and the client can begin to develop an aware-ness of body postures that accompany feelings of being flooded or overwhelmed as well as body postures that accompany a sense of being in control, feeling like an adult, or being able to contain affect. Together, the therapist and client can verbally describe the "flooded" postures and the "in control" postures.

2. Ask the client to give the two postures ("flooded" and "in con-trol") names that are descriptive of the ego states the postures reflect. For example, clients have called the "flooded" posture "overwhelmed," "terror," and "out of it" and have called the "in control" posture "my adult self," "alert and awake," and "grounded."

3. Have the client practice the "in control" posture by verbally describing its particulars. Ask the client to exaggerate the pos-ture slightly. The client will want to make the posture distinct and memorable. This can be done by verbalizing the distin-guishing features of the posture while taking on the posture. For example, "My eyes are open, my spine is erect, I am looking at something in front of me, my feet are flat on the ground, and my breathing is nice and steady." If the client is unable to find a posture reflective of being in control, the therapist and client can create a posture that reflects the elements of grounding described above.

4. Have the client identify nonverbal indicators of feeling flooded that would warrant assuming the "in control" posture. The cli-ent may want to make a list of the indicators.

5. The client may draw a picture or collage of the "in control" posture.

Providing Outlets for Affect

At times, containment strategies are not helpful and the client feels a need to externalize or somehow express affect. However, the client may still not be ready to associate the affect with the knowledge or memories of abusive experiences. In any case, before undertaking memory work, the therapist and client want to be assured that the client has strategies to cope with the expression of intense affect. The strategy, in this situation, is to help the client express the affect in a safe, controlled way. Frequently, the client may not know what emotion she is feeling, but she is aware of a strong pressure to *do something*. Sometimes the survivor experiences free-floating anxiety or a strong urge to act self-destructively (which may be precipitated by the anxiety). The therapist may be able to help the client find a replacement activity that provides some relief while channeling the affect in a more functional way. Strategies for exploring feelings will be covered in the next chapter.

In the early stage of treatment, any body-oriented strategies are aimed at providing psychomotor discharge; the client is not yet ready to connect physical action with feelings. This is a good time for the client to identify physical activities she can undertake when feeling the need outside of therapy to do something or act out. Taking a walk, jogging, doing yoga, or playing racquetball, for example, can provide a great sense of distraction and release. For the client who already has a repertoire of physical activities, the emphasis will be on using the activities as a coping skill. This is a two-step strategy which requires the client to first be aware of the feeling or urge to act out and then engage in a physical activity. For the client who has not already incorporated physical activities into her life, this type of strategy is much more difficult. Some survivors avoid sports or physical activities because of their self-consciousness or discomfort about their bodies; they may not be willing to try exercise until after the sexual abuse trauma has been resolved. In implementing this kind of strategy, the therapist needs to be empathic in evaluating the client's resistance to physical activity. The therapist also needs to be alert to the client who overexercises as a means of avoiding feelings.

Alternatives to Self-Mutilation

As a supervisor and consultant to many therapists over the years, I have found that the single most distressing event for many therapists is their first encounter with a client who is self-mutilating. Many therapists feel scared or helpless and question whether the self-mutilating client should be hospitalized. Although self-mutilation is extremely upsetting to the therapist, if the self-harm is not life-threatening, the client may not need hospitalization.

There are many reasons why clients self-mutilate, including to feel alive, to feel real, to punish themselves, and to feel physical rather than emotional pain (Gil, 1993). Calof (1992) describes self-injurious behavior as a container for affect. In the beginning of therapy, the client is not necessarily prepared to deal with identifying or feeling affect. The client may be disconnected from feelings, disconnected from her body, or unable to tolerate strong feelings. Often the self-mutilating behavior takes place in a dissociative state; as the survivor gains more control over dissociation, becoming more connected with her body, the behavior may become less satisfying and less ego-syntonic. The therapist should thoroughly explore the meaning and function of the self-injurious behavior, as well as identify the behavioral and affective sequence of events leading up to self-mutilation.

The goal is to help the client come up with a strategy to do something different, something that is not self-destructive. For some clients, drawing can be an effective replacement behavior. However, in order for this strategy to work, the client must be motivated to change self-destructive behaviors. She must be willing to forgo the relief that self-destructive behaviors have given her and to find a sense of satisfaction in successfully engaging in more functional kinds of behaviors. The client must be prepared to accept that replacement activities simply will not provide the same kind of satisfaction that she may have received from self-mutilation.

One of my clients had great difficulty giving up beating her thighs. The physical pain of the beating stopped her flashbacks. The only intervention that she was willing to try was holding an ice cube to her neck; she explained that the pain from the cold of the ice was the only thing that was sufficiently distracting to interfere with the traumatic imagery. She had absolutely no interest in trying drawing.

On the other hand, many of my clients have been able to use artwork as a strategy against self-mutilation. Some clients find relief from the kinesthetic activity of drawing, while others find it in the visual images of the artwork. The source of the relief is related to the reason the client self-mutilates.

One Saturday night, to cope with her urge to cut her hand, Felice repeatedly drew a picture of her hand (Figure 16) with bleeding cuts on it; eventually she produced eight drawings. The repetitive action of drawing the same image over and over again resembled the trance-like quality of her self-injurious episodes. She also found some relief in looking at the bright red of the cuts on the paper. When Felice was later hospitalized, she was concerned that the nursing staff would place her on self-injury precautions when they saw her drawings of self-mutilation. We were able to work out a plan with the treatment team whereby she could make the drawings without fear of their being misinterpreted.

Although making drawings of self-injury and suicide may enable the client to avoid acting on such impulses, the therapist must evaluate the client's lethality when encountering morbid or self-destructive images. Such images may be a client's rehearsal of an act or a cry for help. When Joan made a drawing of a figure stabbing herself (Figure 17), we thoroughly discussed her suicidal intentions. The drawing, according to Joan, helped her express her suicidal feelings, providing her with an outlet that diverted her desire to take action against herself. In this case the drawing served as a substitute for the actual act.

Art as an Outlet for Feelings

At times the client will feel overwhelmed by feelings and be unable to verbalize. Providing a safe outlet for the feelings often increases her ability to identify feelings and verbalize. Such a strategy is much like opening a valve on a pressure cooker; the pressure inside the pot comes down to a safe level so that the pot may be opened without fear of an explosion.

Lisa came into a therapy session explaining that she felt anxious and upset. She did not know what to talk about and, in fact, she did not want to talk about anything; she was too consumed with the feeling of anxiety she had awakened with that morning. She said, "There's no point in talking because no matter where I start I keep going round and round." She was willing to draw her

Figure 16   *Drawing of self-mutilation*

Figure 17   *Drawing as an outlet for suicidal feelings*

anxiety. Lisa drew with great energy, drawing large circular patterns. It was clear that as she drew she was discharging some of
her anxiety. When she finished the drawing, she felt calmer; then
she was able to associate to the images in her drawing to describe
her feelings. I suggested that Lisa try drawing her anxiety when
she felt immobilized by it at home. She was able to do this with
some success.

I often have clients make a list of things they can do when they
are feeling overwhelmed at home. Physical activity, relaxation
exercises, and artwork are all good outlets for intense feelings. A
client may purchase a sketchpad for coping with hard times. The
drawings can provide a release and/or distraction and then can
be brought into the therapy sessions for more intensive work on
the feelings depicted by the drawings.

Joan was able to use drawing at home to meet her need to "get
all this stuff out and make it be seen." With no previous experience

Figure 18   *"Out of control"*

with art before working with me, Joan was able to employ art as an outlet for her feelings, which were often overwhelming. She found that making art channeled her feelings, sometimes preventing self-destructive behavior. Joan entitled the drawing in Figure 18 "Out of Control." In our therapy session she described how she drew the intense and confusing feelings she was experiencing, gaining some sense of relief once the drawing was finished. The artmaking gave Joan a sense of catharsis while concretizing feelings that had seemed elusive; Joan gained a feeling of being in control by drawing her feeling of being out of control. In her discussion of the drawing, Joan recognized that she usually defended against her feelings of being out of control, as represented by the colors, with depression, as represented by the black around the edges.

8
CONNECTING BODY AND MIND

THE TASK OF CONNECTING body and mind may involve a long and indirect route, depending on the severity of the dissociative split that has taken place as a result of the childhood trauma. At times it will seem that the survivor is resistant to making the connection. The dissociative split served to protect the child/victim from the horror of her reality; to connect mind and body is to connect with the pain. It is one of the cruel paradoxes of recovery from sexual abuse that the survivor will often feel worse before she feels better. In order to recover she must experience some of the pain of the past.

Fortunately, there are often rewards to doing this work. For one, the survivor who has disconnected from the body has tuned out the pleasure with the pain; the connection restores the survivor's ability to feel pleasurable experiences. For another, connection of body and mind brings the survivor into the present. As long as the dissociative split remains, the pain of the past is as powerful as if it were happening in the present and the ability consistently to experience the world as an adult is lost.

Feeling Feelings

Often, what is behind the client's inability to feel feelings is the fear of losing control. As many of the clinical examples I will describe show, often experiences from the past have prevented the client from feeling safe about expressing emotion. It is helpful to explore the client's fears about expressing feelings. I have asked many clients to draw pictures of what their feelings would look like if they expressed them. Images of "going crazy," tornadoes, volcanoes, and nuclear bombs are not uncommon. No wonder they have been unable to express their feelings! The image of the client's feelings may be used to find a way to express feelings safely. The client may be able to image feeling a tolerable quantity of her feelings or creating an environment that can safely contain her feelings. The therapist may need to remind the client of containment strategies and to go slowly in reconnecting the client with affect.

Many survivors are unaware of having any feelings, particularly sadness and anger. As one of my clients said to me, "I feel spacey now, so I must really be feeling anger." The disconnection between mind and body prevents the survivor from noticing any changes in the body that signal affects.

The fact that the survivor is unaware of her feelings does not mean that they do not exist. Often feelings are expressed in nonverbal behavior. A client may laugh when describing a sad event or shift her posture just before describing an angering one. As awareness of nonverbal behavior is incorporated into the therapy, the client and therapist may begin to decipher the client's unconscious manner of experiencing feelings.

To build an awareness of feelings, I use a five-step strategy that is based on a synthesis of Perls' (Perls, Hefferline, & Goodman, 1977) approach to being aware of the body in the here-and-now and Gendlin's (1981) technique called "focusing." This strategy can be used to gain insight about naturalistic movement (postures, gestures, and movements) and the body-felt sense (sensations in the body that accompany emotions).

Step 1: Paying Attention to the Body

Simply being still and focusing inward on the body may be difficult. Many survivors have used elaborate defenses to avoid feeling and noticing the body, such as dissociation, intellectualization, and denial. An overly busy life with constant crises may also protect the survivor from being in touch with her body. Additionally, some survivors experience flashbacks when they become relaxed or loosen their hypervigilance on external stimuli. Only when the survivor has learned some containment skills is she ready to turn her attention inward. The client's anxiety will ease as she develops a sense of confidence in her ability to gain control over flooding.

Step 2: Identification

By bringing her attention into specific areas of the body, the client begins to develop a less diffuse sense of self. The act of focusing her attention on a particular body location helps the survivor become more attuned to herself and better able to distinguish different types of body sensations. For example, she may discover that not all bodily sensations trigger flashbacks or cause anxiety.

The act of identifying postures, gestures, and movements serves to crystallize nonverbal behavior, making it more distinct and clear. Locating and identifying the body-felt sense is more complex, as the client and therapist may have no apparent cues as to where the sensation may be found. Authentic emotions are usually felt in the torso area. A client describing feelings in hands, feet, or head is probably still disconnected from feelings. Anger is most likely to be felt in the abdominal area. (See Chapter 12 for more on anger.) Sadness is usually felt in the chest area. An appropriate situation in which to explore the body-felt sense occurs when a client, who may be either cut off from or overwhelmed by feelings, expresses some degree of emotion, such as sadness. For the flooded client, the experience of locating the feeling in the body serves to differentiate sensations that have become generalized and resulted in flooding. For the disconnected client, locating the smallest inkling of a feeling increases her overall awareness.

Hyde and Watson (1990) described a technique for reconnecting the body whereby clients locate a feeling in their bodies, place their hands over the location, and breathe into the location until images form. Placing the hands over the feeling gives the client a concrete connection with the body, while breathing provides access to feelings and memories. Breathing also presents the survivor with internal body-centered sensations on which to focus. The path of the breath through the inner body and the resulting muscular movement may put the survivor in touch with affect-laden

FEELING FEELINGS THROUGH THE BODY-FELT SELF

This technique builds awareness of feelings. It may be used when a client who has difficulty consistently connecting with feelings expresses some feelings. It may also be used when a client describes a potentially affect-laden event, issue, or situation with no affect. In that case, the client is to concentrate on the abdominal and chest area, noticing any changes or sensations, however mild.

1. *Paying attention*
   Have the client be still and focus on the sensations in her body that accompany feelings.

2. *Location*
   The client finds a location in her body where she feels the feelings.

3. *Clarification*
   The client concentrates on the location and describes sensations and feelings.
   If sensations are in the hands, feet, head, or other distal parts of the body, ask the client if the feeling goes to any other place in the body.
   Have the client describe the sensation in detail, using as many adjectives as possible.
   If the client is unable to verbalize the sensation because it is too undefined, have her place her hands on the body directly above the location of the sensation and imagine breathing through her hands to the location. Have her describe any sensations.
   If the client is unable to verbalize the sensation because it is undefined or because she cannot find the words, ask her to draw a picture of the feelings in her body (a good homework assignment). This may also give information as to how the feelings are blocked or covering other feelings.

4. *Exploration*
   The client associates to the sensations, the words, and/or the drawing.
   If appropriate, the therapist may ask, "Have you felt this way any time in the past?"

5. *Learning*
   Process the experience with the client, having the client make any relevant connections with the past.

body parts, including the mouth, throat, chest, abdomen, and pelvis. (Techniques for retrieving memories using breathing will be discussed in Chapter 11.)

An awareness of the body-felt sense can be developed by asking the client to notice the internal sensations in her body when she describes any emotional feeling. Most clients can feel some feelings, especially in connection to events unrelated to their abuse. For example, when Lisa stated that she was angry at her roommate, I asked her where in her body she felt the anger. She was able to identify a feeling in her stomach. The identification of a body part and physical sensation associated with her anger enabled Lisa to recognize feelings of anger outside of therapy. The ability to identify feelings gives the survivor more information, which may lead to more choices. When Lisa realized that her roommate's frequent borrowing of her food made her angry, she considered whether the issue was important enough to require a discussion with her roommate. According to Lisa, in the past she would tune out her anger most of the time and then suddenly explode.

Step 3: Clarification

Once the client has located naturalistic movement or the body-felt sense, she can describe it qualitatively using adjectives, images, and metaphors. The goal is to verbalize the essence of the body information. The client may describe the body characteristics very concretely or quite abstractly. For naturalistic movement, the client can recreate the movement or posture, exaggerating it somewhat in order to give it clarity. A drawing of the body-felt sense may provide a deeper understanding or make the feeling more real for the disconnected client and more manageable for the flooded client.

Step 4: Exploration

During the exploration phase, the client makes associations to the naturalistic movement or the body-felt sense. The therapist may facilitate a bridge to the past by asking, "Does this remind you of anything?" or "Was there a time in the past when you felt this way?" The client may spontaneously make associations;

usually when a client becomes familiar with the process, she may, in fact, soon be able to lead herself through the steps. The exploratory phase may simply confirm the survivor's new connection between body and mind or it may lead to insights about current or past issues. If the client has made a drawing, she may gain further information or clarification by associating to it.

Step 5: Learning

Once the client has identified and verbalized body-focused feelings, useful information can be gathered to further the working through of the relevant issues in therapy. The identification of a feeling through a posture or the description of a body-felt sense related to an emotion may: (1) reveal information about traumatic events; (2) uncover resistances to expression of affect; (3) lead to a deeper sense of connection between intellect and emotions and; (4) facilitate the client's ability to recognize feelings independently. The client may discover over time that particular movements or body-felt senses recur, suggesting a theme.

The Age of a Posture

If the therapist suspects that naturalistic movement, particularly a posture, is regressive, she may ask the client, "How old do you feel in the posture?" The following clinical vignette illustrates one client's experience with identifying the age of a posture.

Georgia had been in therapy for about nine months. At a session just before her birthday she was reminded of her eighth birthday, which occurred soon after the death of her mother. As she related the story of her eighth birthday she hugged herself tightly but otherwise showed no emotion. She stated that she felt nothing about the death of her mother—she wished she *could* feel something. At that point, I asked her if she had noticed her posture—the way she had been hugging herself as she talked about her mother. She had not. I asked her to try the posture again, which she did. I then asked her to notice how she felt in the posture. She said she felt nothing. I asked her how old she felt in the posture. Quite quickly she replied, "Little. I feel little." Spontaneously, she remembered sitting at a table at her eighth birthday party, wanting to cry but telling herself she could not because her aunt, who had made the party, would feel bad. In the next session, Georgia reported that she had cried for the first time in many years on the morning of her birthday, when she remembered the grief-stricken eight-year-old who would not let herself cry because she was protecting the adults in her family. She then proceeded to cry what she described as "buckets" over the death of her mother. Having learned some containing strategies, she decided that she had had enough after one day of being so grief-stricken that she was unable to go to work; she was able to put her sadness away until the next therapy session.

A posture can be a powerful tool in eliciting memories and feelings. As the example with Georgia shows, the client needs to know some containment strategies before encountering emotions that have been silenced since childhood. Asking how old the client feels in a particular posture can yield much information as to how a current difficulty is linked with the traumatic experiences of the past. This is the time in the therapy for the client to identify and explore her own naturalistic movement, whereas during the earlier phase the emphasis was on using imposed movement exercises for containment.

Obstacles to Describing the Body-Felt Sense

The Head-Body Split

Not all clients will be able to link nonverbal communication to long-silenced emotions. For these clients, the request to locate or verbally describe bodily sensations may result in the response of feeling nothing. Often there is a blockage in the flow of energy between the head and the body, which may even be visible to the therapist. This block in connection is labeled by movement therapists as a head-body split. In a head-body split, the head may appear quite active when the patient talks, while the body appears flaccid or still. It is as if all the energy is stored in the head and there is a barrier preventing the flow of energy from traveling downward throughout the body. The client with a head-body split may present with intellectualized defenses and have great difficulty feeling or expressing emotions. As clients with a head-body split

INTERPRETING UNCONSCIOUS BODY LANGUAGE

This exercise may be used when:

(a) the client seems disconnected from affect but exhibits a gesture or posture while verbalizing a potentially affect-laden event; or
(b) the client is ready to explore movement characteristics as listed in the Checklist in Chapter 4.

1. *Identification*
The therapist points out or describes the naturalistic movement behavior to the client and they discuss the client's awareness or lack of awareness of such behavior.

2. *Paying attention*
The client takes on the behavior and focuses her attention on her body, noticing any thoughts and feelings that are elicited.

3. *Clarification*
The client describes what she feels when taking on the movement. If feelings are elicited, process them. If no feelings are elicited, ask the client to exaggerate the naturalistic movement.

4. *Exploration*
If no feelings are elicited after exaggerating the movement, ask her how old she feels in the naturalistic movement. Another strategy is to ask the client if the naturalistic movement reminds her of anything.

If the client has no associations, ask her to draw a picture of herself exhibiting the behavior and then describe how she looks in the drawing. Other elements in the drawing, such as colors or line quality, may also be used to elicit associations.

If the exercise is tried in a group and the client has no associations or feelings, group members may try the naturalistic movement and describe their associations and feelings to the client, who may then decide if any of the associations and feelings fit for her.

5. *Learning*
Process the experience with the client and, if appropriate, put it in the context of larger issues in the therapy.

NOTE: Steps 3, 4, and 5 may occur together spontaneously.

begin to develop some awareness of the body-felt self, they may describe their inability to express feelings with images, such as "having a stopper right in my neck" or "something in my throat that stops the feelings from coming out."

Another area of the body that may appear blocked is the chest. The therapist may be able to see that the chest area is extremely rigid or overly flaccid. The extreme rigidity seen across the chest area is called "bound flow," which means that energy is prevented from flowing freely through the body (Dell, 1977). Since flow is reflective of emotion (North, 1972), bound flow may be indicative of blocked emotions; a flaccid chest may also indicate that the flow of feelings is being blocked, as the lack of energy in the chest is such that the emotions are unable to penetrate to the area. The bound chest and the flaccid chest each describe defensive styles for coping with emotions.

The client's inability to feel any bodily emotions due to body blocks will parallel her defensive structure. Because the blockage of tension flow through the body may be characterologic or long-standing, the therapist needs to respect the client's defenses and recognize that the client may not be ready to feel feelings. When the client is unable to locate or describe the body-felt sense, asking her to draw her body showing any obstacles to her feeling emotions may reveal the location of body splits, blocks, or defenses. The client who is ungrounded, has a head-body split, or is a shallow breather often does not feel emotions in the body or feels them in the distal parts where they are mere shadows of genuine emotion. Lack of grounding may serve as a defense against feeling emotions. The head-body split not only prevents energy from traveling downward from the head to the body, but also prevents energy from traveling upward from the body to be verbalized through speech. In other words, thoughts are blocked from being transformed into emotions and emotions are blocked from being transformed into verbal expression.

Inability to Verbalize

For some clients, verbalizing feelings is a new and unfamiliar experience. For the client who is unable to come up with words to describe body information, the therapist may make suggestions based on her observations. The therapist must carefully monitor the client's responses to her suggestions, so that the client does not prematurely accept the therapist's description. The client must resonate with the suggested verbal description, but not adopt it wholesale. An inaccurate verbal suggestion by the therapist may trigger the client's discovery of a fitting verbalization. Alternatively, the client's drawing of the internal feeling may facilitate verbalization; the client can describe the images in the drawing to determine if they fit her bodily feelings.

Case Vignette: Tracy

When the client is ready to begin feeling feelings, the state of tension flow through the chest area may become a focus of therapeutic work. Because this tension flow may be characterologic or long-standing, a single intervention is not likely to miraculously change it; however, it can serve as a beginning. Often, a context in which the chest area becomes relevant is when the client begins to express some anxiety about having people in her life who care about her, including the therapist. The issue of trust may rear its head once again, as it may continue to do throughout therapy. If the client has successfully strengthened her coping skills, she will have begun to be more discriminating about friends, choosing more supportive and accepting individuals as part of her support network. However, the new kind of relationships the client has been developing, including the relationship with her therapist, may cause feelings of anxiety in response to the unfamiliar level of intimacy.

Tracy found herself in just such a dilemma. In the following case dialogue, we explored Tracy's new feelings of affection for a friend, her fear about having such feelings, and the connection with the past:

Tracy: I am beginning to believe that Becky really cares about me and I think I care about her, but I can't really feel anything. I would like to feel something.
SLS: I want you to think about Becky and tune in to your body, noticing any feelings that you might have.

Tracy: (*Closes her eyes*) Nothing. I feel nothing.

SLS: Last week you told me about the gift Becky gave you for Christmas and how it touched you. I would like you to remember how you felt when you opened the gift. Notice how you were feeling. I want you to also notice where in your body you are feeling the feelings.

Tracy: Near my heart. I felt something near my heart.

SLS: Pay attention to that feeling near your heart. Tell me what it feels like.

Tracy: It feels warm and tingly.

SLS: And where does that warm and tingly feeling come from? How does it get to the place near your heart?

Tracy: I'm not sure. I saw the gift and the feeling just was there near my heart.

SLS: Maybe you can trace how it got from the gift to near your heart. Did it travel from your head? From your stomach? How did it get there?

Tracy: I think it got there from my chest. It was like this feeling of love jumped in.

SLS: How did it get in?

Tracy: Oh, I see your point. How did it get in? I haven't let much in for a long time. It's been like I was closed off.

SLS: Where in your body do you feel closed off?

Tracy: In my chest. Yeah. That's it. In my chest. It's like nothing can get in there but somehow the feeling about the gift got in.

SLS: Go back to feeling the warm tingling feeling. When have you felt that feeling before in your life?

Tracy: (*Eyes are still closed*) With my father.

SLS: Did anything happen to that feeling for your father when he left? (*Tracy's father abandoned his family when she was five years old*)

Tracy: I don't know, but I think I never had it again.

SLS: What do you think stopped you from having it again?

Tracy: I couldn't bear to love someone and have them leave me again. I didn't want to care about anybody after that. I think I just closed the door on any feelings of love.

SLS: What do you think about having the door closed?

Tracy: It's hard, but I want to have people I care about in my life. I think I'm ready to be more open to caring, but it's hard.

SLS: What's hard?

Tracy: I feel scared. I don't know why, but this is really hard.

SLS: Yes, it is. It is hard to care about someone when you are so afraid of being hurt again.

Eventually, Tracy came to understand that, despite her fears, she did want to have close, caring friends. In therapy she worked on differentiating her responses to her friends from her feelings of the past. The barrier to feeling affection slowly began to break down.

Case Vignette: Jane

Jane, who said she was feeling something but did not know what she was feeling, had a tendency to flee from her feelings through overactivity. As I asked her to focus on the feelings, identify where they were located in her body, and verbally describe them, she began to connect with her feelings of sadness:

SLS: I want you to just sit with your feelings and focus your attention on them. Notice where in your body the feelings are located. Although you do not know what they are, you are aware of some feelings and you can focus on them.

Jane: (*Closes eyes and lowers head slightly toward her chest*) This is tough.

SLS: What's tough about it?

Jane: I can't sit still. Because the feeling is in my hands and feet. I just want to get up and run away.

SLS: Tell me about the feeling in your hands and feet.

Jane: It's like a tingling sensation, but more like a vibration. Like they want to just start shaking or something.

SLS: Is there any other part of your body that has the tingling, vibrating sensation?

Jane: (*Pause*) Yes. My chest.

SLS: Tell me about your chest.

Jane: It feels shaky.

SLS: Focus on the shaky feeling in your chest. Really notice how it feels. Now describe to me what the shaky feeling is like in more detail.

Jane: It's slowing down a little. It's more like a fluttering now, a fluttering in my chest. There are two parts to the flutter. Like an up part and a down part. On the down part, there is another feeling, when the flutter gets closer to my chest. It almost feels like there is some kind of intense feeling under there and the flutter is covering it or touching it when it comes down.

SLS: I want you to focus on the place under the flutter. Stay tuned in to the feeling when the flutter is on the down part. You can go under the flutter and stay there and see what's there.

Jane: I'm not sure I want to stay there. It doesn't feel good.

SLS: Tell me more about it.

Jane: The feeling. It's a feeling that I never want to have. I think if I feel the feeling I will start crying and I will never stop. I need to stop now.

SLS: Okay. Let's talk about what just happened.

Jane was able to identify the role her overactivity and anxiety played in protecting her from feeling her sadness. The fluttering sensation she felt in her chest was actually her breathing (the "up part" and the "down part" were the movements of inhalation and the exhalation), reflecting the way that physical action hid her feelings. Although Jane was not ready to feel sadness, she was willing to explore the meaning of her body-felt sense and prepare herself to feel the sadness, which she was able to do in a matter of weeks.

Artwork can serve to make feelings concrete and real for the survivor, counteracting dissociative defenses that often result in an amnesia for such moments of connection. I had Jane draw a picture of the sensations in her chest area as she prepared to work on feeling sadness. The image was of a large brown and black avalanche. Jane's associations to the drawing further identified the feelings of sadness and depression. Because Jane was afraid of being overwhelmed by the avalanche of feelings, we worked on containment.

An important question in leading the survivor to identify feelings is: "What color is the sensation?" If Jane had not come up with any more information, I would have asked her while she was concentrating, "What color is the shaky feeling?" Often a color association can lead the client to identification of an emotional feeling.

Understandably, the survivor may resist reconnecting body and mind. The therapist must help the survivor explore the implications of feeling feelings and uncover the meaning of resistances. Usually the resistances are related to early beliefs, early family conflicts, or traumatic experiences.

Somatization

It is not unusual to see survivors in therapy who have undiagnosable physical disorders. I have seen several clients who sought treatment for medical problems only to be told by physicians, usually after numerous tests and examinations, that they could find nothing wrong. I believe that these clients genuinely experienced physical pain and that their abusive pasts were the source of their difficulties. There is some support in the literature for this perspective (Courtois, 1988).

CONNECTING SOMATIC SYMPTOMS

1. Have the client describe the pain of her somatic symptoms, using adjectives.

2. Ask the client to choose a color that describes her pain. Here the therapist should use the client's words, for example, "What color is the burning feeling" or "If the burning feeling had a color, what would it be?"

3. Tell the client she is going to find an image which describes her symptom. The color and the adjectives that describe the pain will help her create an image. The client may have already described an image when she identified a color.

4. Use the image to help the client find some meaning about the symptom. Have the client associate to the image. Drawing the image may be helpful.

Linking the body and mind is an often long and arduous process for the somatic client. Frequently, the somatic client is unable to tolerate the time and/or the work of psychotherapy because her frame of reference has been the medical model of taking a pill or having surgery, a remedy which quickly cures the patient and requires little effort on her part. Nonverbal modalities may begin to make the link between somatic problems, the emotions, and abusive experiences. Imagery may bridge physical pain and emotions, a technique originally used by behavioral psychologists.

When using nonverbal techniques, both therapist and client need to maintain a sense of perspective by placing the techniques in the context of long-term therapy rather than seeing them as instant symptom relief (which they will not be!). It is important to recognize that nothing should be used as a replacement for medical treatment. However, as I stated before, some survivors are unable to find a medical explanation for their ailments, despite numerous consultations with medical experts.

Helen suffered from undiagnosable pain in her throat. She described the pain as a constant gnawing. She saw the pain as a black monster that was eating away at her and described the monster as evil. She then recognized that she herself felt evil; her shame was eating away at her. Helen said she had secretly thought this about herself but she had never before told anyone or connected the pain with her shame. This insight only briefly alleviated Helen's pain, but it did help her to talk more about feelings and issues that she had been keeping secret.

Rebuilding Body Awareness

The numbing experienced by many survivors in relation to their bodies seems to thaw slowly in the course of therapy. The client may try several tasks and activities outside of the therapy sessions to support rebuilding positive body awareness and body esteem. Classes in Feldenkreis and Alexander technique, yoga, t'ai chi, and breathing provide an opportunity to focus on body awareness while improving strength and flexibility. More intrusive kinds of body work, such as deep tissue massage, have the potential to trigger flashbacks. Once a survivor has resolved the sexual abuse trauma, massage may be a valuable experience in reconnecting with the body; however, it is contraindicated until the survivor has developed good skills in differentiating the past from the present and in coping with flashbacks. There are a growing number of massage practitioners who are trained to work with survivors.

Self-Touch

Some survivors can distinctly remember the time when their bodies went numb. With the numbing, many tasks of girlhood and adolescence that nurture the body were avoided or neglected. In reconnecting, the survivor may redo many of the earlier developmental tasks centered on the body. The therapist should not take for granted that the client, as a matter of course, incorporates nurturing grooming activities. Self-touch may be particularly problematic, especially for the survivor who self-mutilates. I recommend that a client who has been uncomfortable with self-touch or grooming try some of the following activities:

- applying hair conditioner
- brushing the hair for 100 strokes
- applying moisture cream on the hands
- applying moisture cream on the feet
- applying moisture cream on the entire body
- a facial (self-administered)
- self-massage

The focus of these activities is practicing a prolonged, gentle touch. I recommend that the client do these activities for herself rather than have someone do them to her; at this point the focus is on the survivor's feeling a sense of control over her body as well as learning to self-nurture herself. The therapist needs to evaluate if such activities stimulate self-punitive responses. If the survivor is having difficulty with these tasks, the introduction of neutral images and associations to touching may override negative memories or associations. For instance, the client may be reminded to touch herself as if stroking a cat or touching a smooth marble floor. The goal is to find an image which has no negative associations and reinforces a neutral, gentle touch.

9
CREATIVE PROBLEM-SOLVING

ONE OF THE MORE TRYING experiences in psychotherapy for both therapist and client is the phenomenon of being stuck. Stuckness typically occurs when the client is unable to make progress around a particular issue or see any resolution to a particular problem. Two areas around which I have frequently encountered stuckness are turbulent romantic relationships and feelings of guilt or shame over sexually abusive experiences.

While stuckness may reflect a client's need to make changes at a slow pace, many survivors experience cognitive distortions in their thinking that impede problem-solving (Jehu, Klassen, & Gazan, 1985–1986). One type of distortion that lends itself particularly well to using nonverbal modalities and is found quite frequently among survivors is personalization, which occurs when the survivor takes responsibility for things that were not her fault. Jehu et al. provide a more extensive list of cognitive distortions and discuss verbal techniques aimed at cognitive restructuring for survivors. Here I will focus on nonverbal techniques that may be used to transform distorted thinking.

Distancing

The object of distancing is to shift from a subjective to an objective stance. Art, movement, and imagery all provide distancing through the use of symbols. The client may draw a picture, allowing herself to view her difficulty. She may create a stylized movement that depicts a problem. She may develop an image that represents a conflict. Once a problem is translated into a symbol, distance is achieved. The symbol offers the possibility of new learning about the problem, as well as the opportunity for generating solutions. Distancing circumvents the survivor's habitual patterns of thinking about herself, patterns that may be replete with self-blame and low self-esteem.

Drawing

The task of drawing a picture of herself as a child or looking at childhood photographs gives the survivor the distance from which to view herself with compassion. The objectivity of the drawing or photo may spark the recognition that she was truly an innocent and helpless child. Survivors who think of themselves negatively, with adjectives such as "bad" or "evil," may begin to replace those ideas. For instance, Diana, who was unrelentingly self-blaming about her sexual abuse, was able to feel kindly toward herself for the first time when she drew a picture of herself at the age when she was first abused. Looking at the picture, she remarked that she appeared scared and little; she saw herself as defenseless and blameless. Although Diana did not consistently maintain this perspective toward herself, she was able to lessen her self-blame when reminded by the picture.

Drawing with the nondominant hand (Capacchione, 1988) adds further distance and can help the perfectionistic and/or self-critical survivor who is resistant to drawing. Diminished motor control over the nondominant hand often produces childlike line quality, increasing its effectiveness as a representation of the innocent child. This technique may also be used to stimulate memories (see Chapter 11).

Dreams

Another technique that relies on distancing as a means of problem solving is dream interpretation. Dream symbols, particularly in dealing with romantic relationships, often provide the distance necessary for clients to view the unhealthy aspects of relationships without the idealization, protection, or caretaking that they may impose on the lover or spouse. Conflicts in the relationship may be apparent from dream material, so that the client is able to discover the conflict for herself; this relieves the therapist from trying to point out problems, which often results in resistance from the client or tension in the therapeutic relationship. In working with dreams, the client may draw or role-play significant parts of the dream. I often have the client focus on taking on the posture of a person in a dream in order to better identify the person's thoughts and feelings.

Sheryl had a dream about riding on the back of a motorcycle that was being driven by her boyfriend, Joe. The motorcycle was out of control. Afraid the cycle would crash, she looked for a helmet but could not find one.

Sheryl had been living with Joe for six months. He was constantly critical of Sheryl, who was financially supporting both of them. Despite coming into therapy week after week tearfully complaining about Joe, she refused to see anything wrong with him, always making an excuse for his behavior, such as "he had a bad day." My efforts to point out the cruelty of Joe's behavior only led Sheryl to become angry or defensive. Although she had several dreams that may have been interpreted as reflecting problems with Joe, it took a dream in which the symbols were less abstract for her to begin to gain some insight about the relationship.

I had Sheryl turn her chair around and imagine that she was sitting on the back of the motorcycle. She described how she was feeling: "I am hanging onto Joe for dear life. I'm terrified—terrified that I am going to lose him and terrified that we are going to crash. All I can do is hang on." Sheryl acknowledged that getting hurt was inevitable, given the current state of the relationship. She was then able to begin to work on the problem with Joe from the point of view of seeing herself get hurt rather than acting as Joe's protector.

Dreams also offer the opportunity to generate creative solutions. The client may create alternative endings to dreams, which depict empowerment or resolution. Such endings may lead to actualization outside of the therapy or may simply give the client the opportunity to internalize positive possibilities. Before the client recreates the ending of a dream, the feelings and affects expressed by the dream should be examined; recreating an ending should not be used to avoid painful or intense feelings unless the client is in need of containment.

In Sheryl's alternative ending a motorcycle expert with a huge crane hauled the motorcycle to a repair shop before there was an accident. She then saw couples therapy as a real-life equivalent of going into the repair shop. To give her a sense of realistic expectations, I had her describe all the possible things that might happen to the motorcycle in the repair shop, including being broken beyond repair. One of the outcomes of this discussion was that Sheryl recognized her desire to have someone else solve her problems rather than having to take responsibility for herself.

One pitfall of creating new endings is that the client may become hopeless about her current situation if she formulates a miraculous ending for her dream. She may see her life as offering no such miracles and then become frustrated, angry, or depressed. There are two possible approaches to take if this occurs. The first is to investigate whether the seemingly miraculous ending contains some aspect of problem solving that could be translated into a real-life solution. In the case of Sheryl's dream, the realistic solution was going to couples therapy. The second approach is to process with the client what it means that she has chosen an ending that involves being rescued by a miracle. One of my clients, Myra, had a dream about being kidnapped by a bear. In her new ending, she described angels coming to rescue her. It turned out that when she was being sexually abused as a child, Myra dissociated by staring at a painting that had angels in it, imagining that they were rescuing her. This knowledge helped Myra begin to understand her desire to be rescued, her anger when she was not, and her need to begin to develop a sense of empowerment in her adult life.

Sometimes a dream element may become a symbol representing a recurrent theme in a client's life. Sheryl returned to the image of a motorcycle many times during her therapy. Almost a year after the motorcycle dream, Sheryl ended the relationship with Joe after finding out that he was having an affair with her friend. Reflecting on the dream, she decided that before she got on another motorcycle she would make sure she had a helmet and a chance to thoroughly check out the safety of the motorcycle and the driving

WORKING WITH DREAM SYMBOLS

1. I recommend that the client keep a pencil and paper by her bed to record dreams. Lying quietly after awakening in a relaxed state helps bring dream images to consciousness. The facility to remember dreams seems to improve with practice.
2. Have the client choose and describe the dream that is the most interesting or significant to her.
3. If the client is in the dream, have her work on the role she played in it. If she is not in the dream but there are people in it, have her choose the most dominant person or the person with whom she most identifies. If there are no people, ask her to choose the element or object that is the most interesting or prominent. If a dream is complex with many events, have her choose one event in the dream.
4. Have the client role play the dream person or object. She can do this by first arranging her posture to represent the posture of the person/object. If the person/object is moving, have her move as it would. Ask her to identify feelings and thoughts of the person/object while in the posture/movement. The therapist can help the client get involved in the role by asking questions. The client should be made aware that she can use her imagination to embellish her role. For instance, if she is in a car, the therapist can ask her where she is going and what will happen when she gets there.
5. If a problem is being faced by the person/object, have the client create a solution. She may need to be reminded that she can use her imagination to develop a solution. Have the client create a posture or movement reflecting the solution. Ask the client to describe her thoughts and feelings in the posture/movement.
6. Process with the client, identifying similarities to the client's life. Explore whether the solution offers any hints to resolving a real-life dilemma. Explore the possible meaning of the solution. Even if no parallels with the client's life are obvious, the solution may reveal whether she sees herself as active or passive, helpless or powerful, or victim or survivor.
7. The entire process can be repeated with other elements, people, or objects in the dream.
8. The client may want to make a drawing or collage representing significant symbols from the dream work.

NOTE: A variation is to have the client move from the dream posture/movement to the solution posture/movement, exploring the transitional movement for clues as to how the solution may be reached.

record of the driver. Sheryl had moved in with Joe after knowing him for only two months; she realized that she needed to get to know more about a prospective live-in boyfriend before she got seriously involved. As a reminder to herself to be more self-protective around men, she made a collage about motorcycles and found a place to hang it in her bedroom. The metaphor of the motorcycle dream gave Sheryl the opportunity to circumvent her defensiveness and to discover a new way to approach relationships with men.

Activating the Imagination

When I am working with a client who has an especially difficult time coming up with any kind of positive outcome to a problem, I may encourage her to let her imagination run wild—to formulate *any* solution to the problem, no matter how far-fetched—and then to draw a picture of the solution. Suggesting that the client write a movie script sometimes gives her the objective shift she needs in order to become more creative. Supporting an actively working imagination begins to combat the passivity that accompanies feelings of hopelessness and powerlessness, even if the client is not yet ready to take action. The existence of a drawing of an imagined solution may provide a sense of object constancy, which the client may be unable to maintain by merely relying on her imagination.

Problem-Solving Through Movement

Another problem-solving technique relies on body postures or movements as symbols of a problem and its solution. Kelly had been depressed for several months and appeared to be making no progress in therapy. I asked her to create a posture or movement that represented her feelings of depression. She positioned herself face down on the floor with her arms at her side. I then asked her to create a posture or movement that represented how she would like to feel. She felt too uncomfortable moving (which is often the case), so she created a standing posture with arms reaching for the ceiling, face uplifted. I then asked her to move from her first position on the floor, to the standing position, paying attention

PROBLEM-SOLVING THROUGH MOVEMENT

This exercise is appropriate when a client feels stuck and is able to identify a goal but is unable to make progress toward that goal.

1. Have the client visualize a posture or movement that represents her current situation.

2. Have the client visualize a posture or movement that represents a goal or a change.

3. Now have the client actually make the posture or movement that represents the goal. To reinforce and clarify the posture or movement, have the client verbally describe how she feels in the posture/movement. Support the client in fully experiencing the posture/movement and the feelings associated with it.

4. Now have the client do the posture/movement for her current situation. Again, support the client in fully experiencing the posture/movement and the feelings associated with it.

5. There may be enough material elicited from the two posture/gestures to warrant verbal processing before continuing.

6. From the posture/gesture of the current situation, ask the client to find a way to move from that posture/gesture to the goal posture/gesture. Have the client verbalize any thoughts or feelings that arise during this process.

7. The process of changing from the first posture/gesture to the second may contain metaphoric or symbolic images that will contribute to the client's understanding of the feelings or issues that are standing in the way of her making progress. The client's verbalizations of the experience of trying to move from one posture to the next may provide language descriptive of the underlying issues. Sometimes even very concrete descriptions of the transition offer the potential for insights and new learning.

NOTE: For the client who is too uncomfortable trying full body movements or postures, there are two alternatives: (a) suggest that the client make the two postures while sitting in her chair; (b) suggest that the client make movements or gestures with her hands while sitting in her chair.

to what it takes to get from one posture to the next. Kelly silently lay on the floor for a full minute, finally explaining, "I can't get up myself. I need you to pick me up." This discovery led to Kelly's identifying her feelings of anger and dependency toward me. The process of concretely moving from one symbolic posture to another often brings to the surface underlying issues that have stood in the way of problem resolution.

10

A FEW WORDS ABOUT MULTIPLE PERSONALITY DISORDER

ALTHOUGH THE PERCENTAGE of sexual abuse survivors who experience MPD is unknown, a high percentage of those diagnosed with MPD have a history of sexual abuse (Boor, 1982; Coons & Milstein, 1984; Putnam, Guroff, Silberman, Barban, & Post, 1986; Wilbur, 1984). Gil has advised: "When adult survivors present with a history of severe, chronic, bizarre, or ritualistic abuse, or evidence of dissociative states (current or past), the therapist must assess for the presence of multiple personality disorder" (1988, p. 154). The therapist treating sexual abuse survivors should familiarize herself with the literature on MPD. Among the more practical books available is Putnam's (1989) *Diagnosis and Treatment of Multiple Personality Disorder*. The therapist inexperienced with MPD should seek supervision, consultation, and/or training in treating MPD and should consider referring the client to a clinician with expertise in treating dissociative disorders.

The diagnostic criteria of multiple personality disorder as described by the *Diagnostic and Statistical Manual of Mental Disorders, 3rd Edition, Revised (DSM-III-R)* * (APA, 1987) consist of the following:

1. The existence within the person of two or more distinct personalities or personality states (each with its own rela-

---

*At the time this book was written, *DSM-IV* was not yet available. However, the *DSM-IV Draft Criteria* (APA, 1993) renames multiple personality disorder as dissociative identity disorder and this term will most likely be adopted in the final version of *DSM-IV*.

tively enduring pattern of perceiving, relating to, and thinking about the environment and self).

2. At least two of these personalities or alter states recurrently take full control of the person's behavior. (p. 272)

Although in many respects the treatment of individuals with MPD resembles treatment with abuse survivors, the existence of many personalities or ego states requires specialized strategies. Specifically, the therapist will need to build a therapeutic alliance with many alters and facilitate communication among them. It is not uncommon to discover an alter who cannot use verbal communication because he/she is an infant, is unable to speak English, or is handicapped. The nonverbal modalities, especially art, have the potential to hold an unusually prominent role in the treatment of MPD.

The Use of Movement

There are few resources describing the specific nonverbal indicators of MPD, although it has been generally accepted that personalities may vary in their body language. Three studies that used highly technical, systematized approaches to movement observation of MPD individuals found that distinctly different movement patterns accompanied different personalities (DeArment, 1993; Kluft, Poteat, & Kluft, 1986; McCoubrey, 1990). However, these changes are not necessarily apparent to the untrained observer and may not be apparent without repeatedly viewing movement behaviors on videotape. I have observed switching between personalities both with obvious movement indicators and without any observable change in movement. When the switching is obvious, some conspicuous nonverbal signs are an abrupt jerk of the neck and a fleeting contorted facial expression. I have also seen a brief moment of stillness just prior to switching, which was confirmed by DeArment's (1993) study of movement characteristics of one individual with MPD. Any dramatic shifts in body language or posturing style should alert the therapist to the possibility of multiplicity.

With regard to treatment, body-oriented interventions have not been widely employed, probably because of the extreme lack of connection with the body that accompanies dissociative disorders, as well as the negative feelings many MPD clients have about their bodies. Movement therapists have had some success using structured movement groups as an adjunctive therapy (Baum, 1991, 1993; Sutherland, 1991). Edith Baum (1991, 1993) describes the goals of movement therapy groups with MPD members as: (1) to establish trust through kinesthetic empathy; (2) to negotiate social interaction; (3) to elicit self-expression and traumatic material; (4) and to develop a more coherent sense of self. A typical group format involves group members spontaneously moving to music.

The expression of movement facilitates interpersonal as well as intrapsychic experience. For example, group members may feel a greater sense of acceptance and acknowledgment when their movements are mirrored by other members of the group. A member may experience catharsis through movement, as well as improved integration because of a greater sense of connection with the body. Movements of group members often reflect their progress in therapy, with nonverbal behavior frequently preceding verbal behavior (Schmais, 1974). A hand gesture extending outward from the mouth may appear just before a client is ready to tell her story of abuse; a gathering movement of the arms starting near the abdominal area and reaching upward may signal an approaching integration (Elizabeth Templeton, personal communication, March 1, 1993).

For the nonspecialist therapist, body-oriented interventions as described throughout this book may be used with some cautions and adaptations. The highly dissociated survivor is unlikely to maintain her attention on body-centered sensations, especially during early and stressful phases of the therapy. To the extent that she senses a body that is not real, an MPD client with rapid switching or distinct alter personalities will show unusual distortions in body image. For instance, child alters may deny the presence of breasts or eyeglasses. In such situations, body-centered information may be used to learn more about a particular alter, i.e., how that alter perceives herself. The recognition of particular body states that accompany ego states may provide valuable information and eventually facilitate integration. On the other hand, the MPD client's extreme body image distortion may limit the use of interventions that rely on body awareness until the later phases of therapy.

I have discovered that grounding techniques are quite helpful with multiples. A growing awareness of the body builds on the survivor's ability to be present as herself in the here and now. As with any client, the success the MPD client has in using grounding techniques will be dependent on her motivation and comfort level with remaining in the present. At certain points in treatment, the survivor may consciously try to prevent switching or dissociation, especially as a new response to traumatic triggers or as an effort to process traumatic material.

The Use of Art

Art therapy has been called a primary modality for this population (Turkus, 1990). Art can help with diagnosis as well as further the progress of therapy. The nonspecialist therapist should see art indicators as reason to further investigate a diagnosis of MPD, leaving the actual diagnosis through art to the trained art therapist.

Assessment

In addition to the specific art indicators discussed below, there are particular contents or symbols that may be suggestive of MPD. The presence of an additional figure in a drawing, sometimes seen next to or near a figure that obviously represents the client, may suggest the existence of an alter personality (Gil, 1991). Distinctly different artistic styles appearing consistently over time may represent the work of different alters, each having an individualistic style or different developmental ability. I once worked with an MPD client who was a trained artist; one alter drew in a very impressionistic style while another drew realistic, representational art. Alter personalities have been found to show different styles of art, poetry, music, and handwriting (Schultz, Braun, & Kluft, 1985). Child alters produce developmentally immature, childlike art. According to Fuhrman (1993):

> While at particular times the artwork of MPD patients reflects developmental characteristics that parallel their current chronologi-

cal age, it is not uncommon to find that adult MPD patients age regress in their artwork. This is apparent as line quality becomes less controlled, spatial organization deteriorates, and images become more generalized. (p. 28)

The most comprehensive study of MPD art characteristics done to date used the Diagnostic Drawing Series (DDS) (Cohen, Hammer, & Singer, 1988) and compared MPD artwork with the artwork of individuals diagnosed with major depression, schizophrenia, borderline personality disorder, and a control group with no psychiatric diagnosis (Mills & Cohen, 1993). The DDS, which has standardized instructions and uses standardized art materials, consists of three drawings: a tree drawing, a free drawing, and a feeling drawing. The study was able to differentiate the art of MPD subjects from other diagnostic groups and controls.

Several graphic indicators emerged in the artwork of MPD subjects: movement, odd trees, disintegration, tilt, abstraction, and enclosure. Movement "is characterized by dynamically drawn abstractions or by depictions of actual movement" (Mills & Cohen, 1993, p. 46). Odd trees showed one of four characteristics in tree drawings: "(a) branches falling apart from trunks; (b) chaotic branches; (c) unrecognizable trees; and (d) trees with trunks of minimal lengths" (p. 46). Disintegration refers to a lack of relationship and coherence in the picture, either in theme or visual elements. Tilt exists when the vertical axis of an image is tilted 15 degrees or more. Other elements which were found in MPD artwork are: art containing enclosures consisting of repeated outlines, containers, or barriers; and use of color that is idiosyncratic and unmodulated.

The authors caution against relying on any single sign:

Any of the elements described above could occur in the artwork of any person. However, the appearance in a DDS of a cluster of structural signs, in conjunction with certain elements of theme and content, should raise the clinician's index of suspicion and prompt further investigation. (Mills & Cohen, 1993, p. 59)

Treatment

Art with MPD clients may provide valuable information about the underlying system of multiplicity, facilitate communication among alters, and uncover traumatic material (Cohen & Cox, 1989; Jacobson, 1993; Jacobson & Mills, 1992; Spaletto, 1993; Spring, 1993). The client may draw a system picture or a drawing that maps the system giving information about the relationships among alters and about the function and age of alters. An observing alter or "watcher" who is aware of most of the alters may draw the picture or assist in its production, as well as verbally explain its contents. One of my clients drew a stunning system picture that depicted 23 alters. The client explained that she had been unable to fit all 37 alters in the drawing. A system picture may not necessarily reflect an accurate number of alters; in addition to the artistic limitations mentioned by my client, as therapy unfolds more alters may become known who have not been accessible to the watcher alter.

There is a danger that the therapist may reinforce separation rather than integration in the way that she discusses artwork produced by alters. Frye and Gannon (1990) give sound advice for using accurate and carefully chosen language in viewing and discussing artwork to help the patient talk about and accept the reality of disowned images:

> "Did *you* make this or did someone else?" or "I know *you* didn't do this, so-and-so alter did . . . " invite disclaimers of denial. Even though it is cumbersome to say continually, "The part of you that drew this," or "You drew this even though you don't remember doing it," it is vital not to promote splitting and disownership. (p. 6)

I have found art helpful in communicating messages to and reinforcing alliances with alter personalities. Maureen had a persecutory alter she called Mo who hated being in the hospital on weekends and attempted to run away several times. As part of building an alliance with her, I had suggested that she get involved with taking care of the plants in the greenhouse, as she had mentioned her love of gardening during our intake interview. Drawing on a hidden caretaking side of the persecutory personality, the intervention was surprisingly successful. (This occurred after many fruitless efforts at suggesting activities that might interest her as a diversion from self-destructive activities.) Each time she tried to run away, she had felt that no one cared about her. She was, however, extremely concerned as to who would take care of the plants in her absence.

Discussion revealed that Maureen had a complicated emotional attachment to plants from childhood, similar to the kind of attachment children often have to pets. This led to the discovery of a more vulnerable side to Mo. I suggested that she draw a picture of her favorite plants and hang it in her room. The drawing accessed the caretaking part of the alter at times when she might not have been otherwise available. With the help of the nursing staff, verbal and visual reminders of plants assisted the client in getting through the weekend without incident.

A drawing may simultaneously allow the involvement of several alters, facilitating integration and cooperation. The identification of different symbols, colors, and styles particular to specific alters may facilitate the client's acceptance of the MPD diagnosis. Self-portraits of various alters may reflect the age, gender, and personality differences of alters, breaking down the client's denial of the diagnosis. Figure 19 shows a collage Joan made when she was grappling with the diagnosis of MPD and was ready to discuss it in therapy. The creation of the collage gave her a format in which to organize her many conflicting feelings about the diagnosis. While the images and headlines suggest the internal confusion that she felt, artmaking gave her a way to externalize the experience.

A strategy I have used to facilitate communication among alters is to have the client draw a picture reflecting improved communication. Sometimes the client comes up with her own image of communication; when she has no image of her own, I suggest an image depicting all the personalities sitting around a conference table holding a meeting.

Alters who hold childhood memories may draw pictures that graphically depict traumatic events. In this way, art can act as a bridge across amnestic barriers, allowing information to be transmitted among personalities, facilitating integration. Many MPD clients lack the verbal language to describe their experiences, which may be more readily depicted through art. The therapist needs to carefully assess whether other parts of the system are ready to handle the knowledge of such images or if the pictures are serving a cathartic need for the alter drawing them. Saving the

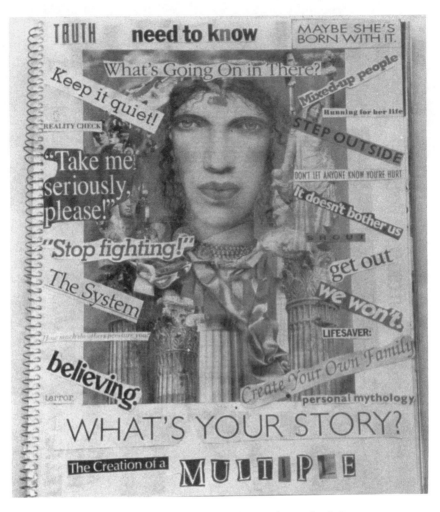

Figure 19   *"The making of a multiple"*

discussion of drawings until other personalities have begun to process memories and the client has shown the capacity to utilize coping skills is generally advised.

I have discovered that the visible display of art supplies is often inviting to child alters. This has both advantages and disadvantages. For example, with one client I suspected multiplicity but had not yet observed any alter personalities. Just prior to a session with her I had bought a large new box of markers and inadvertently placed it on my desk. A child alter appeared "to play" and asked to draw with the markers. I was then able to contract with this alter to participate in therapy. A less positive situation occurred when another client's child alter literally took over the treatment hour in order to draw. I eventually discovered that this alter appeared only when my art supplies were visible; I began to put them in a closet before her sessions and was thus able to modulate her presence until other strategies were effective.

Nonverbal modalities frequently give voice to material that remains unconscious to the individual with MPD. Alter personalities can communicate through artwork and can make their presence known through differences in body movement. Traumatic material may leak through amnestic barriers, presenting itself in art images and in gestures or postures: A watcher alter or a child alter may draw trauma pictures; alters who were present during abuse may reenact traumatic episodes with body movements. Although all survivors express unconscious material through nonverbal modes, the MPD client potentially presents a greater amount of submerged material. The therapist must decide whether the client will be best served by working on containment, exploration, or expression, sharing nonverbal information accordingly.

11
MEMORY WORK

EDUCATING THE SURVIVOR about the need for preparation and safety in working with memories will maximize the possibility of a positive therapeutic experience. Pacing the process is an important aspect of doing memory work. Although planned memory work is the ideal, clients may spontaneously begin to recall traumatic memories through flashbacks in the midst of a therapy session. Faced with the decision to contain the memory or proceed with an abreaction, the therapist should curtail memory work if any of the following contraindications exist (Steele & Colrain, 1990):

1. the early stages of therapy
2. an unstable therapeutic alliance
3. current and ongoing abuse
4. extreme age, severe physical infirmity, and/or terminal illness
5. lack of ego strength, including severe borderline and psychotic states or pathological regression
6. insufficient time in the therapy session
7. insufficient preparation for abreactive work
8. client not committed to follow-through in the therapy
9. therapist not sufficiently grounded in knowledge and skills to manage the process

In the event that the therapist determines that memory work is contraindicated, the strategies used for coping with flashbacks are helpful with containment (see Chapter 5). Having the client take on a grounded posture with eye contact, focusing on being in the here and now, may curtail an abreaction. As anyone who has been faced with a highly dissociated client in the midst of a spontaneous abreaction well knows, the therapist may need to try any number of strategies before finding one that works. Suggestive statements based on hypnotic strategies may be helpful, such as "On the count of three, you will open your eyes and be here in my office with me." Once the therapist has the client's attention, suggesting that she maintain a grounded posture may prevent her slipping back into a dissociative state; many clients are unaware of the enormous influence that body posture has on the ability to stay in the present. Moving around in the office may help the client break the dissociative spell while simultaneously focusing on here and now sensory information, such as the feel of the floor under her feet, the color of the curtains, etc.

Retrieval of traumatic memories may be the catalyst for a powerful chain of events that leads toward integration and assimilation of the sexual abuse trauma (Courtois, 1988, 1992; Dolan, 1991; Gil, 1993; Herman, 1992; McCann & Pearlman, 1990; Meiselman, 1990; Steele & Colrain, 1990). The major components of memory work, which often overlap, are as follows:

1. retrieving traumatic memories
2. abreaction
3. recontextualizing the meaning of the abuse
4. reassessing feelings toward family members
5. realignment of the survivor's sense of self

Once the survivor has the coping skills and ego strength with which to handle recalling the sexual abuse, she may focus on remembering (Courtois, 1992; McCann & Pearlman, 1990). She will next work toward connecting feelings with the knowledge of the sexual abuse trauma gained from memories, an experience called abreaction (Breuer & Freud, 1957; Lindemann, 1944). A recontextualization of the sexual abuse trauma occurs when the survivor is able to look back into the past and correct distorted thinking about the abuse or make new meaning from remembering. Memories may facilitate new learning through such insights as the survivor's recognition of her authentic helplessness as a child or the abuser's power and authority as an adult or trusted loved one.

Recontextualization of the abuse has a multidimensional impact on the survivor. She may begin to see herself and others differently. She may view her perpetrator as abusive for the first time, causing her a great sense of loss or rage over losing her image of a loving or protective adult. The shattering of her illusions about family, relatives, or friends has the double-edged effect of freeing her from her own sense of guilt while implicating others who may have been viewed as innocent or neutral. She may be faced with the prospect of dealing with her perpetrator and family in the present, causing her to consider the issues of disclosure and confrontation. Her realization that the abuse truly occurred may trigger an existential crisis, raising questions such as, "How could such an awful thing happen to an innocent child?" The resulting realignment of the survivor's sense of self is usually well worth the struggle; the survivor may emerge from memory work freed from old images and beliefs about herself, ready to devote psychic energy to her development as a worthwhile adult.

Safe Remembering

Once the therapist and client agree that memory work is in order, the process of safe remembering is facilitated by preparing the client, structuring the experience, and using distancing techniques (Courtois, 1992; Dolan, 1991; Gil, 1993; Steele & Colrain, 1990).

Preparation

Remembering has the potential to unleash strong emotional and behavioral responses even when the experience is therapeutic. Not only may there be an exacerbation of PTSD symptoms, but the survivor may feel exhausted, rageful, or grief-stricken as a result of the work of remembering. Planning for remembering allows the survivor to feel a greater sense of safety and control. A longer session of an hour and a half may be scheduled for memory work, since retrieving and processing memories often require more time than the usual 50-minute hour (Courtois, 1992). Planning should involve explicit discussion of the mechanics of maintaining safety both inside and outside the therapy. The emphasis of planning is not to alarm the survivor about the results of remembering, but to remind her that she is now an adult who has many more resources with which to face the painful memories of the past than she had as a child. For instance, with the knowledge that she was going to begin working on memories in the next session, Georgia was able to arrange for her sister to pick up her children after school and make them dinner. She had a friend drive her to the therapy session. After a session of remembering, Janet planned to go to an AA meeting and then go out for coffee with her sponsor. She had the number of a 24-hour crisis line if needed. Both Georgia and Janet were able to draw on supports, in contrast to the isolation they experienced as children.

Preparation also includes defining the particulars of what helps the client feel safe in the session. Sitting on the floor, closing the curtains, and wearing a special necklace are examples of behaviors that have given survivors a sense of safety and security in doing memory work.

Another aspect of maintaining safety involves establishing clear methods of communication when the survivor is in the midst of remembering. Because many survivors may have strong affective responses, the therapist may need to know when the survivor is simply experiencing profound emotion that is a necessary accompaniment to abreaction and when the survivor feels out of control and in need of the therapist's help in pacing the experience. One of my clients, Jean, usually sobbed quite deeply whenever she felt emotion. She would appear to become overwhelmed by her crying and was quite nonverbal at these points. In preparation for memory work, we discussed how we could maintain contact so that I would know she was feeling safe and she could let me know if she needed my intervention. She decided that she would shake her head vigorously in a "yes" movement if she needed my help in modulating her emotional response. The therapist should assess whether her need to modulate the intensity of emotion during an abreaction is a result of her own countertransference reaction or of the client's genuine need for containment. Perhaps more than any other part of therapy with survivors, witnessing the survivor's profound emotion in the midst of remembering can be heartrending work for the therapist.

An important piece of preparation involves the client's exploring her expectations of what will happen if she remembers. The discussion should include anticipated feelings and behaviors both inside and outside the therapy. The survivor may envision several different scenarios, each with a different outcome. Exploration of the client's fears about remembering will not only identify areas where more work is indicated but also assist her in developing strategies to address her fears. For instance, Jean was afraid that she would pass out while remembering. In preparing, she identified symptoms that would signal that she was going to pass out and agreed that we would stop the memory work at any hint of the specified symptoms. She found a posture that helped her feel more stable, minimizing the potential of any injury to herself if she fell from passing out. (Much to my relief, she was able to complete memory work without passing out.)

Structure

Another key to successful memory work is the use of structure in the session. Because of the survivor's potential to regress into the timelessness of the past, structuring the experience serves as an anchor to the present. Structure is created through having a clear beginning, middle, and end to the therapy session and to the sequence of memory fragments. The therapist plays an active role in providing structure. Because the survivor may be in a dissociative state during memory work, the therapist's voice serves as an important anchor and is the instrument that describes the structure of the session.

An initial structuring technique is to explain the planned order of events in the session. For example, the therapist might explain: "First we'll talk about what we are going to do today and make plans for after the session. Then we'll work on some memories. At the end of the session we'll make sure we have time to talk about what happened and how you are feeling."

As the client is relating memory fragments, the therapist describes a sequence of the events, echoing the survivor's verbalizations. Memory gaps are included in the sequencing. For example, after the client has recounted a memory fragment, the therapist may say: "First the lights went out, then you are not sure what happened. The next thing you remember is. . . . " Structure paces the session and gives the survivor a sense of connection with the present.

Distancing

Distancing techniques ensure that the survivor will not be retraumatized by experiencing memories as if they were actually happening to her in the present. Distancing provides two major functions: (1) to prevent the survivor from being pulled into the past as a child; and (2) to keep the abuse from being reenacted to the survivor's body.

The survivor wants to return to the past with her adult observing ego. She may watch the abuse happen to her child-self, but she does not want to become the child and reexperience the trauma. Direct and indirect techniques will facilitate the survivor's maintaining her adult presence. The therapist may actually explain to the client that she is going to go back to the past and see what happened to her as a child. A classic distancing technique used in hypnosis is often useful: The client sees the events of the past unfold on an imaginary TV or movie screen. Drawings also provide distance; the traumatic events are happening on the page rather than directly to the survivor (Gil, 1993).

The subtleties of language may provide a sense of distance. Describing traumatic events in the past tense and the third person may minimize the intensity of memories (Steele & Colrain, 1990). For example, "First he slapped me," allows greater psychological distance than "Now he is slapping me." "She (the child-self) felt so alone and scared," offers more protection than "I feel so alone and scared."

Another distancing strategy is for the survivor to maintain an adult body posture, sitting with her feet on the ground. By making a conscious effort to use the "adult body posture" described in Chapter 7, she may be aware that her body is in the present and only her mind has gone back to the past. Body postures and positions may be discussed as part of the preparatory phase in order to assist the client in identifying postures that reinforce safety and grounding. The use of postures to facilitate remembering are discussed below.

In addition to body postures, a number of devices may help to anchor the survivor in the present and remind her of feelings of safety while doing memory work. So-called "power" tokens, such as clothing and jewelry, may evoke feelings of strength and safety. Phyllis wore a crystal necklace to her memory session. Jean's best friend made her a "Power T-shirt," which was decorated with healing symbols. June dressed in purple because she believed the color gave her energy and power. Elaine drew an elaborate picture of herself as a "Woman Warrior" and kept it in her lap during memory work. Visual and kinesthetic cues will reinforce the survivor's experience of being an adult as she journeys back to the past of her childhood.

Although many survivors have had multiple incidents of abuse, they do not necessarily have to remember and process all of them (Dolan, 1991). The therapist can suggest to the client that one incident will represent many incidents. This can be very reassuring. Generally, having one incident represent many seems to be most effective when there are a number of similar incidents with the same perpetrator. However, "representative abuse memories must be captured with enough associated affect to process the trauma in some detail and to work it through" (Courtois, 1992, p. 16).

There appears to be great variability among survivors with regard to the amount of time needed to fully process memories and the number of times they need to go through the process with different types of memories. At the minimum, memory work occurs over a period of weeks. The client who continuously works on memories and is in a constant state of emotional distress needs help evaluating whether there is a way to lay memories to rest, at least temporarily. Memory work seems to be complete when the survivor can talk about the trauma with some affect but without too much distress, is no longer experiencing flashbacks, has achieved a new sense of meaning about the abuse, and is feeling hopeful about the future (Steele & Colrain, 1990).

Memory Retrieval Techniques

Recent controversy about the reliability of abuse memories (Comstock, 1993; Kluft, 1992; Loftus, 1993) suggests caution in eliciting memories. Although I generally believe my clients' stories of abuse, the backlash against the survivor movement makes clients and therapists more vulnerable to criticism and disbelief. By asking indirect rather than leading questions, the therapist is less likely to influence the survivor's recollection of the past. For example, instead of asking, "Was it *your father* who was in the room with you?" the therapist may inquire, "*Who* was in the room with you?" I concur with Courtois (1991) that the therapist has a responsibility to ask the client if she was ever sexually abused, but after the initial response I generally allow any further discussion of the topic to come from the client.

Memory is a variable and unpredictable thing. I have witnessed the emergence of long-repressed memories when the survivor finally felt safe enough to focus on remembering. I have also seen elaborate and dramatic efforts at remembering fail despite the best efforts of both therapist and survivor. I am a firm believer that people remember when they are ready to remember. However, there may be some circumstances that will frustrate the best efforts at readiness. For instance, the scant research on memory has shown that very early and violent abuse is more likely to result in amnesia than later, less violent abuse (Briere & Conte, 1993; Herman & Schatzow, 1987).

The process of remembering is idiosyncratic. Memories return in pieces and in different sensory modalities (Briere & Courtois, 1992; Courtois, 1992). Some survivors approach memory work with a storehouse of previously retrieved memories from dreams, flashbacks, journal-writing, and artwork. In the early phases of therapy, when the principal goal is for the survivor to maintain functioning when faced with a memory, this storehouse may have been unexplored. Now these previously undigested memories are the focus of therapy. Some clients approach memory work with little or no previous recall of traumatic events. I have worked with a number of clients who have given no indication that they were having memories or flashbacks; yet, when they were ready to work on the trauma, they have revealed detailed memories that they have quietly kept to themselves.

One of the first steps in memory retrieval work is to assess what the survivor already remembers. Memories exist temporally, over time, and multidimensionally, across the four BASK dimensions (Braun, 1988a, 1988b). The BASK model of dissociation accounts for the separation of experiential components during a traumatic experience. The survivor may find herself with incomplete memories that lack one or more of the BASK components: *behavior*, *affect*, *sensation*, and *knowledge*. The BASK model has particular implications for integrating nonverbal material into the process of remembering. Behavior may exist in the form of repetitive postures, gestures, or movements that the survivor seems to make unconsciously, out of context, or in response to stress. Affect is represented by the survivor's feelings, which, because they are split off from the rest of the BASK continuum, may appear incongruous to situations. Sensation resides in body memories, which often appear to have no connection to present experience. Knowledge appears in the survivor's ability to recount the details of what happened. Behavior, affect, and sensation are the body's way of knowing, while knowledge is the mind's way; this dichotomy represents the mind-body split so frequently experienced by survivors.

An assessment of the survivor's memory components according to the BASK model will indicate which aspects require additional retrieval and integration work. For example, one of the more commonly observed manifestations of missing BASK components occurs when the survivor recounts the events of the traumatic episode with no affect. In this case, the survivor is displaying knowledge without affect, suggesting to the therapist that questions need to be directed to the affective realm during memory work.

Because of the split between emotions and knowledge, some clients may be quite capable of retrieving a complete memory with little affect unless the therapist asks feeling-focused questions. It is possible to modulate the work to a certain degree, so that the client focuses on knowledge or affect, depending on the kinds of questions the therapist asks. For example, asking "How did you feel?" will elicit a different kind of response from "What happened next?" In going after affective responses, the therapist needs to be aware that she is leading the client toward an abreaction.

Given the client's vulnerability and the therapist's ability to influence the therapy, the therapist and client need to work collaboratively in directing the flow of the therapy. This will facilitate successful resolution of remembering. The session may focus on evaluating what the survivor remembers or on processing memories. Although the therapist and client have some ability to influence the focus of remembering, both should be aware that strong affect may be experienced by the client at any point during memory work.

Art and Memory

A number of art techniques may facilitate the retrieval of memories and the consolidation of what is already in active memory. Art may be produced outside the session, as long as the client does not become overwhelmed by flashbacks, intrusive memories, or flooding of emotion. The therapy session may then be used to process the content of the art, clarify the chronology of events, connect with affect, and integrate.

Time-Line

Developing a chronology of events beginning with the client's earliest memory is a structured way to assemble a history. A time-line may be constructed on a large sheet of paper (computer fan-fold paper allows the client to make a long time-line that can be easily folded into a portable size). The client draws a line across the page and fills in dates of remembered events. Memory blanks are left unlabeled. Once the chronological events are filled in, an affective component may be added to the time-line by the use of colors to highlight, shade, and outline time periods. Particular colors may represent certain feeling states or attitudes toward life events. The survivor who resonates with art may draw symbols or images to accompany specific life events.

Cohen (1992) describes a life-mural consisting of drawings of memories executed as the memories emerge during therapy. The drawings may be taped together to form a continuous chronology and folded along the taped seams for storage. I have found this to be especially useful both with inpatients who retrieve a great number of memories over a short period of time and with outpatients who retrieve memories over a period of weeks, months, or years. The drawing project gives the memories a context by creating a chronology, provides a record of events for future processing, and offers the client an activity for unstructured time.

Flashbacks, Dreams, and Nightmares

Once the survivor has decided to work on memories, dreams and flashbacks become the focus of exploration. Because drawings of dream fragments and flashback images may provide valuable information about the past, the client is encouraged to keep a sketchbook for drawing at home; the drawings may be processed in the therapy sessions. The survivor may now review drawings made in the earlier phases of therapy for the presence of traumatic material.

Rhoda had made a series of drawings to help her cope with flashbacks. At the time she made the drawings, her purpose was to release anxiety and focus on some external activity. A later review of her work revealed that the abstract drawings were of sexual organs, which was not initially apparent. At that time of the flashbacks, Rhoda was not ready to explore the context in which she may have encountered sexual organs. During memory work, the images provided a starting point from which she could talk about the abuse.

Sandra drew a dream fragment (Figure 20), which was the word "slut" carved into her wrist with a razor. She brought the drawing into therapy. In eliciting Sandra's associations to the drawing, I asked, "Who called you a slut?" Sandra tearfully identified her perpetrator for the first time. Although she had not repressed the memory of her abuse, she had not been ready to talk about it in therapy until the session. In making a drawing from a dream, the survivor is able to unconsciously choose the symbol(s) that is most meaningful to her. Processing the image may result in making conscious previously repressed or verbally inaccessible material, leading to new insights.

Floor Plan

Eliana Gil (1988) has suggested that the survivor draw the floor plan of her childhood house and take the therapist on a tour. Memories may be triggered through visual and kinesthetic descriptions of furnishings, along with other sensory experiences such as fragrances. The floor plan facilitates distancing, as the client is actually looking down on the house rather than being enclosed by it. However, the act of describing the house may very well cause

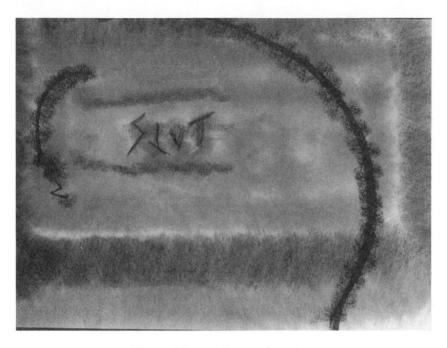

Figure 20   *Dream fragment*

the survivor to feel as if she is in it rather than looking down; in that case the therapist may want to suggest the use of the past tense to give some distance.

Enter the Drawing

The client may literally enter a picture to discover the past, provided she uses distancing and safety techniques. Over a weekend, Sonia had a flashback and immediately made a drawing of an image from it, a blue dresser. Because we were working on remembering in therapy, she decided that she was ready to learn more from the flashback rather than merely surviving it as she had in the past. Realizing that she needed some support to do this work at home by herself, she imagined herself walking into the drawing accompanied by me. Entering the drawing, she saw for the first time that her aunt was present during a molestation by her uncle. She then forgot about the memory until she came to her next therapy session, where she was able to process the memory. Sonia was able to use distancing, by imagining that I was coming into the drawing with her, and containment, by rerepressing the memory until the therapy session. Obviously, not everyone will be able to handle the lack of distance that going into a drawing creates, especially outside of a therapy session. However, as clients progress in therapy, particularly if they have already had some experience with memory work, the capacity for independently retrieving memories increases. As discussed previously, many survivors experience several rounds of remembering as part of the cyclical nature of healing from sexual abuse (Bass & Davis, 1989; Courtois, 1991; Sgroi, 1989).

Draw Yourself as a Child

Drawing a picture of herself as a child at the age of the abuse (Steele & Colrain, 1990) may allow the survivor to reconnect with her childhood self, thus triggering memories. Photographs, as well as drawings, of the survivor as a child may give her distance from her self-blaming adult self; the accompanying lifting of guilt, however brief, sometimes allows new memories to emerge.

For the client who is perfectionistic about drawing or has anxiety about her artistic skill, drawing with the nondominant hand (Capacchione, 1988) gives additional distance to the drawing of the childhood self.

I often ask clients to describe the little girl in the picture: What is she like? How does she feel? What is she thinking? The little girl can literally take on a life of her own, coming alive for many clients. Sometimes this happens spontaneously through the use of the drawing. When the story of the abuse is told by the child in the drawing, the client has more distance from the events of the past. The child in the drawing offers the opportunity for the story of the past to be told in the third person; for example, "She said this happened first and then that happened."

Kinetic Family Drawing

Exploring the Kinetic Family Drawing (Burns & Kaufman, 1970) has the potential of contributing missing information about the past as well as jogging the survivor's memory. Early in therapy,

Eliza had drawn a KFD which did not include herself, explaining that she was probably in her room. At the outset of therapy, the focus of work on the drawing was on understanding the family dynamics. When we began working on memories, we explored more deeply the motivation for Eliza to stay in her room and how she was *feeling* at that time. The feelings led to recollection of traumatic material:

SLS: What made you want to be in your room?

Eliza: I wanted to be invisible.

SLS: What made you want to be invisible?

Eliza: I felt like I had done something wrong and no one should know.

SLS: Can you tell me more about what that was like for you?

Eliza: It was awful. I felt so alone and so *bad*. I was a bad *girl*. (*At this point Eliza closed her eyes and began to rock slowly.*) I'm a bad girl. I'm really bad. I can't tell anyone what I did. I can't tell.

SLS: Eliza, I want you to see yourself as a little girl on the TV screen like we talked about. Can you see her?

Eliza: (*Shakes her head affirmatively*)

SLS: What is she not supposed to tell?

At this point, Eliza, after some reassurance that she was safe, recounted the story of her abuse. This was a planned memory session, for which we had prepared for several weeks.

The Body and Memory

The body remembers. A posture, gesture, or kinesthetic sensation may trigger an intense rush of emotion due to its resemblance to the body's past experience. Kinesthetic memories of sexual abuse may include internal physical sensations such as sexual arousal and pain, postures and gestures such as clutching of the pelvis, and feelings such as a panicky sensation in the chest. The survivor may have no words or knowledge with which to make sense of what the body remembers. Because body experience is an internal experience, body memories have the power to pull the survivor into the past, overshadowing the external experience of the present.

Remembering and the subsequent release of affect frequently occur just after or simultaneous with a change in movement, posture, breathing pattern, or muscle tension. The change may range from subtle to quite obvious. The therapist may observe such a change, which gives her the ability to stay present with the client even during times when the client is unable to verbalize. The observant therapist will be able to maintain communication with the client by describing the nonverbal change and asking the client to describe what is happening to her at that point.

Often, caught up in the power of the memory, the client may not be aware that she has made a nonverbal shift. In fact, the client may appear quite dissociated. The therapist, by carefully observing and verbalizing the movement changes in the client, can help anchor the client in the present.

When using body information to retrieve memory material, the therapist needs to be sensitive to the potential for retraumatization. While the survivor's description of body experience as it is occurring may prove to be highly useful for eliciting further knowledge about the abuse, distancing techniques should be used to avoid the survivor's re-experiencing the trauma in her body. While a body memory is a form of re-experiencing, once it is identified as such the client's perspective may be shifted so that further exploration does not lead to further re-experiencing.

Body Memories/Kinesthetic Flashbacks

Kinesthetic flashbacks, also called body memories, represent the physical sensations of the sexual trauma. Because body memories often include pain or sexual arousal, distancing devices are strongly recommended in using body memories during memory retrieval. Body memories may spontaneously occur as the survivor verbally recounts her memories of the abuse. On the other hand, body memories may appear to come out of nowhere. The therapist may observe sudden muscle contractions and signs of physical distress, such as wringing of hands and clutching of the pelvis or stomach.

Placing body memories within the context of the abuse incident and processing the episode sometimes minimize their return as spontaneous flashbacks. As the survivor is experiencing the body memory as part of a planned memory session, the therapist can verbalize the survivor's body experience, using distancing language such as, "You are bent over and clutching your stomach. What was happening to you? Who was with you? What were you thinking?" By pairing a description of the body behavior with other BASK components during questioning, the story of the abuse may be retrieved. It is important to remind the survivor who is in the midst of strong bodily sensations that she is in the here and now. For example, "While your body remembers what happened, you know that your body is really here now. You are safe now because your body is remembering while you are safe here in my office." I may also cue the client to stay grounded in her body during memory work: "Notice your feet on the ground and your back against the chair. Your body is here in my office while you remember."

When the memory is over, the client may want to plan some kind of activity that will be soothing to her body. It is not unusual for body memories to result in pain after the session is completed. Dana complained of pelvic pain for two days after the memory session. She decided to take a bubble bath and use a heating pad. In addition, she asked me for a drawing project; I suggested she draw a picture of her pelvic area looking healed.

When a client describes a body memory that she had outside of the therapy session, I may have her make a drawing of the memory or come up with an image that represents the memory in order to prevent re-experiencing. The distance of the drawing or image allows us to safely explore the kinesthetic experience.

Dissociative Movements and Postures

Some survivors experience the split-off behavior component of the memory in the form of a dissociative movement or posture. A typical behavior is hiding in the closet. The survivor may not know what triggers the behavior, why it is happening, or what events surround the hiding. As part of planned memory work, the postural or gestural element of the behavior may serve as a bridge to memories in much the same way as body memories. Postures with repetitive movements tend to create a dissociative state similar to the state in which the abuse occurred, thus facilitating remembering. While fetal-type postures often represent behavior that followed the abuse, some gestures and postures may actually be directly connected to the abusive event. The therapist can gauge her questioning accordingly.

Paula found herself curled in a ball and rocking whenever she felt afraid. After we prepared for memory work, Paula sat on the floor of my office in her rocking, curled-up posture. I sat on the floor across from her as I asked her to describe her experience. Since my voice was her anchor to the present, I maintained a constant verbal description of what she was doing and saying in response to my questions. Focusing on sensory experience led to Paula's remembering her abuse. After Paula experienced the memory and began to feel a great deal of emotion, I suggested that she move back to the chair so that she could be grounded and process the memory as an adult.

I have used such dissociative movements as cuticle-picking and thumb-sucking to access memories. First I have the client associate to the movement, describing thoughts, feelings, images, and past experiences related to it. If the client's associations are sparse or bland, I may have her exaggerate the movement. The movements or postures frequently developed as an unconscious means of coping with the trauma and can thus be used as an entry point to traumatic memory.

Body Scan

A particular body part may distinguish itself to the client in some way, perhaps by being in pain or by being an area of great dislike. The client may be aware of this on a conscious or semiconscious level. Even when general questions such as "Is there any part of your body that is a problem for you or that seems to cause you extra anxiety?" results in a negative answer, this may not actually be the case. A structured scanning of the body, part by part, may yield information that is less conscious. The therapist can lead the client through each body part, asking questions in order to identify conflictual areas. Starting at the top of the head and working down toward the toes, the therapist guides the client, referring to each body part and asking questions:

Notice your throat. Pay attention to how it feels to you. Notice any sensations. Do any images come to mind when you focus on the throat? How strong or how faint are your feelings, sensations, and images? . . .

After a scan of the entire body, part by part, the client is asked to identify one or two body parts to which she has strong or unusual associations. The client may then explore the associations further. The body part may be brought into greater awareness by placing the hands or an object such as a small pillow or a ball (Hoffman, 1991) on the area while the survivor continues to explore thoughts, feelings, and sensations; the object also has a grounding effect.

Although jaw pain or pelvic pain may appear to be obviously connected to an abusive episode, the client may be completely out of touch with this possibility. The process of scanning enhances the client's awareness (i.e., "Gee, it really does hurt") while putting the body part into context with the rest of the body (i.e., "Maybe it means something that it hurts more than other parts").

Sometimes the identified body part is numb, invisible, or in some way disconnected. The client may be directed to gently and steadily direct her breathing to that body part (Hyde & Watson, 1990). If she has difficulty visualizing the body part in order to direct her breath to it, she may place her hands over the part. As the client continues to breathe and focus on the body part, the therapist asks her to describe her experience. The therapist verbally reflects back to her as a means of grounding and structuring. The client may make a drawing or collage illustrating some aspect of the body experience, including visual images of body parts, feelings, thoughts, or sensations. The art may be concrete or abstract. Awareness of visual images and kinesthetic sensations may further trigger memory.

Regrounding After Remembering

After a memory has been processed, grounding postures will assist the survivor in stopping the abreactive experience and in preparing to resume functioning outside of therapy. A posture that emphasizes a connection with the ground while stressing an upward pull will reinforce being in the here and now as an adult. Walking or sitting while attending to the contact of the feet with the ground and the upward pull of the spine represent such grounding postures.

12
ANGER

ANGER WORK IS PERHAPS the most satisfying *and* terrifying part of the healing process for both client and therapist. For the client to reveal her deeply buried rage and for the therapist to accept and bear witness to such rage is a potentially risky yet transforming experience. While anger containment exercises may be used in the early phase of therapy, anger expression exercises are reserved for the middle and advanced stages of treatment, when the client has developed the ego strength to tolerate the vulnerability of revealing intense anger and the client and therapist have forged a solid therapeutic relationship.

Survivors present a wide array of coping strategies to deal with their anger. They may cope with anger on a continuum from feeling nothing to uncontrollable outbursts of anger or they may alternate between the two extremes. Anger may be misdirected at the self, resulting in self-destructive behaviors. Some survivors who internalize their anger experience headaches, gastrointestinal problems, and other somatic complaints.

Many abused children learn at an early age that anger is a dangerous emotion, as adult displays of anger may lead to abuse of the child. The child's displays of anger may lead to punishment by adults, shameful behaviors by the child, or shaming by adults. For some children, *any* emotion is considered dangerous; in an attempt to protect the self, they become numb to any feeling. Jennifer, for example, explained that she was safest if she was invisible. Expressing any feeling openly made her visible and, therefore, subject to ridicule, punishment, rejection, or further abuse. Jennifer learned at the age of five that anger was too dangerous an emotion for her to feel. She explained, "I just turned myself off."

Anger may be associated with the perpetrator. Janice explained, "If I let myself show anger, then I'll be just like my father" (her perpetrator). She buried her anger deep inside her, suffering from migraine headaches beginning in early adolescence. Joanne, whose alcoholic father molested her, found herself unable to control her fits of rage both as a child and as an adult. She described her angry episodes as "Something I just can't help; they just happen." She was particularly shamed by the way she had "beat up" her younger brother during childhood and she constantly worried that she would abuse her own children. Joanne's fear of her angry behaviors led to self-hatred and depression.

It is not uncommon to hear survivors describe an angry behavior directed toward the self or others and be mystified as to the reason for its occurrence. Therapy helps the survivor to perceive feelings of anger, to identify their sources, and to appropriately and safely express anger. While some survivors may enter treatment experiencing intense anger and need help with anger management, some survivors may show little or no affect and need to become more expressive.

Anger and the Body

Anger is viscerally experienced in the body through involuntary reactions, such as increased muscle tension, increased pulse rate, and increased skin temperature. An adaptive response to anger not only recognizes physiological signs of anger but also identifies the need to de-escalate involuntary reactions through voluntary activities; the individual with an adaptive anger response has a repertoire of "cooling off" activities, which may include verbalizations of anger, sublimation of anger, and calming strategies through self-talk, such as "I'm entitled to my anger, but I don't want to lose control" or "It's not that important."

For the individual who is disconnected from the body, there will be no awareness of the initial physiological responses to anger.

Subsequently, the behaviors which might counter these responses are not routinely undertaken. The result is a body that chronically holds anger, seeking release in a form that becomes part of the individual's unconscious coping style. The release may take the form of somaticization, explosive outbursts, self-destructive behaviors, self-hatred, obsessive-compulsive behaviors, aggressive behaviors, or inward directed anger in the form of depression.

For some survivors the accumulation of anger since childhood produces chronic muscle tension, which is visible to the observant therapist. Anger may be apparent in such manifestations as a clenched jaw or rigidly held muscles throughout the body. One type of body attitude that reflects chronically held anger looks like a tightly coiled spring. Physical activities that would normally provide a release for muscle tension may be ineffective or, in extreme instances, may serve to stimulate the release of violent impulses. The combination of disconnection from the body and chronic tension may result in over-exercising, a drive to find release through increasingly aggressive activities, or uncontrollable outbursts of anger.

Regular physical exercise may begin to provide a routine release of built-up muscle tension. For clients clearly in need of regular physical release, as evidenced by chronic muscle tension and/or expressions of intense anger, I suggest regular exercise. Swimming, aerobics, running, fast walking, and bicycling all allow a safe outward release of energy, providing a channel for pent-up emotion. Competitive sports, such as handball, basketball, racquetball, baseball, and tennis, have the potential for injury for the individual who cannot experience aggression while simultaneously maintaining a good sense of control. Exercise that requires constant muscular contraction, such as body-building or weight lifting, can be helpful for the individual who does not have the control to safely play competitive sports.

A safe physical release of anger involves control over three components: (1) the capacity to direct the anger at a safe object (connectedness); (2) the ability to regulate the intensity of strength used (modulation); (3) the mastery required to end the activity (sequencing). Sports activities provide structure that encompasses the components of safe physical activity. For instance, in basketball, the ball is dribbled and passed through control of direction and strength (connectedness and modulation) and numerous rules dictate the sequence of plays, such as the amount of time the ball can be dribbled by one team and the length of time of the game.

Physical activity may become unsafe when there is a breakdown of controls as a result of a weak structure or the addition of affect. Sports injuries have a tendency to occur when players are distracted by emotions or when rules are lax. In addition, the adult survivor may be prone to difficulties with the three components of control (connection, modulation, and sequencing) due to the nature of some of the most common aftereffects of sexual abuse. In regard to connection, dissociation, which disconnects the survivor from the here and now, may interfere with the capacity to direct energy at a particular object. The ability to modulate strength of movements may be impaired by a lack of awareness of the body. The timelessness of trauma may hinder the survivor's mastery over sequencing, which requires the capacity to self-regulate a beginning, middle, and end to events.

Although there is variability among individual survivors in the degree to which symptoms interfere with control, the emotion of anger has the general effect of decreasing control (which is true for anyone). The potential for losing control in the physical expression of anger suggests guidelines for the therapist:

1. In the early phases of therapy, anger work should be focused on containment. Exploration should not include active movement.
2. Physical discharge of anger should be safely structured through nonaffect-laden activities, such as sports.
3. Interventions for the physical expression and exploration of anger in therapy should be safely structured in the middle and late stages of therapy.

Anger Work in Psychotherapy

The highly motivated client with good ego strength may be able to learn anger containment techniques in the early phase of therapy, while the more fragile client may need more time before she is to be able to use new coping skills when under stress. Novaco (1975) found that with a nonclinical population cognitive

---

ANGER CONTAINMENT EXERCISE #1:
DEEP BREATHING

This exercise can be used to calm a patient down in a session or to rehearse for situations outside of the session during which the survivor is having difficulty controlling anger.

1. The therapist helps the client come up with a simple calming: statement to say to herself when she inhales, such as: "I am breathing in cool, calm air."

2. The client takes five to ten calming breaths while repeating the calming statement.

3. The client may add a calming color to the instructions, giving her an additional focus of concentration, such as: "I am breathing in cool, calm sky-blue air." If the client chooses a highly affect-laden color, such as red, the therapist should process the choice with the client, eliciting associations.

4. It may be helpful for the client to have a cue card to remind her of this technique, such as a 3″ by 5″ index card, which may be carried in the client's wallet or posted at home. The client may write her calming statement herself or have the therapist write it using a colored marker matching the client's calming color.

5. The client should check that the statement feels right for her; if not, she can correct the statement to one that is more comfortable. Trying out the statement may lead to new creative ideas.

---

behavioral techniques, such as self-talk, were more effective in anger management than relaxation training. I have found that survivors often want to do something *active* when angry and have difficulty using self-talk, especially in the early stages of treatment. The negative internalized voices that many survivors experience may overpower cognitive behavioral suggestions relying on internal messages and cues. Both art and movement activities offer external, active interventions that have the potential to override internalized messages, at least temporarily.

For the client who has not yet worked on memories, anger may be randomly experienced or there may be little or no awareness of the object of her anger. The intensity of the anger may be incongruous to the situation or the survivor may be out of touch with the intensity of her anger. Identification of angry feelings, sensations, behaviors, and triggers is the focus of therapeutic work at this point. By making the unconscious conscious through the exploration of art images and nonverbal behavior, the client may begin to gain a greater understanding and mastery of her anger.

An important therapeutic function is to normalize feelings of anger. This can be accomplished by describing the physiological reactions that typically accompany anger and reviewing a variety of responses to anger that range from subtle to blatant, identifying what is socially acceptable and what is not. Without exploring the client's belief system about anger, the therapist should not assume that the client has a good grasp of acceptable means of expressing anger. It is not uncommon to encounter a survivor who feels that if she expresses any anger she will "go over the edge" or totally lose control.

Many survivors are unable to feel angry at their perpetrators. This may be due to various reasons with quite different sources, such as loyalty ties, a disconnection from feelings, a belief that the client is to blame for the abuse, or minimization. One client explained, "How can I get angry at my uncle, when I consider the source?" This kind of dismissal of the client's anger needs to be explored more deeply. Simultaneously, the client needs to feel understood for forgiving the perpetrator or for feeling ties of loyalty. The therapist is placed in the tricky position of accepting the client's attitude toward anger, encouraging a healthy expression of anger, and not letting her own feelings toward the perpetrator predicate how the client is to feel. The therapist needs to be able to understand extreme rage at the perpetrator as well as forgiveness toward the perpetrator. Obviously, resolution of anger is a complex process that will only truly be approached in the late stages of therapy. The client may need to work on anger repeatedly as each new layer of understanding about the actual events of the past is acquired and the past is differentiated from the present.

Many survivors, lacking a sense of self and unable to gain distance from their own experiences, can get angry for others but not for themselves. Group therapy with other survivors may provide an opportunity to feel angry about others' abuse and recognize that similar feelings are appropriate regarding their own situation.

While many details concerning the client's beliefs about expression of anger and experiences with anger will naturally be uncovered as the therapy unfolds, the following questions can serve as a guide in preparing to do deeper work with anger:

- When you are angry, what happens? What do you do?
- Have you ever lost control when angry? If so, how have you lost control?
- Do you recognize anger when you are feeling it?
- How did family members express their anger when you were growing up?
- How do you feel when people close to you (significant other, friends, family) show anger?
- How do you feel about yourself when you express anger?
- What feels like an acceptable or tolerable level of anger as expressed by others?
- What feels like an acceptable or tolerable level of anger as expressed by you?
- When you expressed anger, how have others responded to you? When you were a child? As an adult?
- What do you think would happen if you expressed your anger?
- What situations cause you to get angry or work to control your anger?
- Do you feel any anger about the abuse you experienced as a child? If so, at whom do you feel angry? What would your anger be like if you could express it?
- What would it be like for you to get angry at me (the therapist)?
- How do you feel about showing your anger in front of me?

Depending on the history of the therapeutic relationship, any anger the client has expressed toward the therapist can be discussed in the context of the client's overall experience and beliefs about anger.

When the issue of anger presents itself in the therapy, the therapist needs to decide if the time is right to explore anger further or to work on anger containment. It may be appropriate to assist the client in calming down or gathering factual information rather than focusing on the angry affect. The therapist should undertake exploration or expression of anger only when a good therapeutic alliance has been established and there is sufficient time in the session to fully process the experience; it also may be advisable to postpone anger work if there is about to be an interruption in regularly scheduled therapy sessions (such as the therapist going on vacation). A good rule of thumb is to start anger work only in the first third of the session, allowing sufficient time for processing and de-escalation (Steele & Colrain, 1990).

The same structure and guidelines described in the last chapter for memory work should be applied to anger work. For example, as in preparing for memory work, the therapist and client should designate a signal indicating that the affect has reached an intolerable level for the client, so that containment may then be undertaken. It is of vital importance that the therapist not curtail anger work based on her own intolerance of affect. Anger work should be contained only when the survivor cannot tolerate the intensity of affect or when the client or therapist are in real physical danger. Techniques that actively mobilize the client's anger require that the therapist have a good grasp on containing techniques, is aware of danger signals that may warn of loss of control, and is confident in stopping the intervention if signs point to an impending explosion or acceleration of anger, doing so in a nonshaming and accepting manner.

Art and Anger

Art can provide a safe container for anger, transform angry energy into a creative product, give clues for the client to recognize the depth and intensity of angry feelings, and give opportunities to metaphorically act out revenge fantasies. However, the physical act of drawing may serve to mobilize angry energy, resulting in a loss of control during or after art activities. When the therapist sees a potential for loss of control as a result of art activities, she should initiate a verbal dialogue that explores the client's responses to the artwork in order to assess whether further drawing is contraindicated.

ANGER CONTAINMENT EXERCISE #2:
MY LEFT FOOT*

At times a client may experience unexpected flooding of angry feelings which are seemingly disconnected from external events. This is especially likely when a client has recently uncovered material from memory that affirms either the brutality of the abuse or the lack of protection by adults. This technique is effective when the client is experiencing anger in a very physical way and the client has the ability to use dissociation positively. Although it may be useful to work with the intense feelings of anger in therapy sessions, the intensity of the flooding may be interfering with the client's daily functioning, particularly in a work or school situation. This technique contains flooding of anger outside of the therapy session.

1. The therapist helps the client identify where in her body she is feeling anger.

2. The client attempts to visualize all of her anger moving to her left foot, where it will be stored until she feels free to express it. Stamping the foot or rotating the ankle may reinforce the experience of having all the anger in the foot.

3. The client may feel the need to release some of the anger by stamping the foot.

4. If the client feels free to express her anger or fully experience her anger, either at home or in the therapist's office, the client can envision the anger leaving her foot to return to its original location(s), as identified in Step 1.

5. The client may want to practice moving the anger from the left foot to the rest of the body and back to the foot several times in the session.

NOTE: The left foot is safer than the right foot because the right foot is used to step on the gas pedal in driving. If the client feels an intense feeling of anger, stamping offers some release. This exercise is not recommended for anyone with knee problems.

*This exercise was inspired by "Dissociated containment of post-traumatic stress symptoms" by Yvonne Dolan (1991) and a similar exercise by David Calof (1992).

Creating art may be simultaneously containing and expressive. By projecting her anger onto the art media, the client is channeling angry energy into an adaptive activity that has the potential to contain the flow of anger. At the same time, the creation of art also expresses feelings of anger through the depiction of visual images and facilitates motor discharge through the act of making the art. However, the visual image or motor activity may stimulate further anger, leading to an escalation of anger rather than containment or resolution.

Some indicators of overstimulation of angry affect, potential acting out, or loss of control in artwork (Jacobson, 1986, 1990) are listed below:

1. rips or slashes in the paper
2. images depicting suicidal gestures, homicidal acts, or gestures of self-harm
3. destruction of artwork
4. inability to contain artwork to paper

If such indicators appear in artwork that the client brings into a session, the therapist needs to undertake an exploratory discussion in order to assess whether artwork has precipitated any dangerous acting out behaviors. If the client reports acting out or reports increased stimulation of intrusive thoughts or imagery after the completion of artwork, then independent art production may be contraindicated. If such indicators appear as the client is producing artwork in the session, the therapist needs to immediately assess the client's potential for losing control. If it appears that production of artwork is mobilizing and stimulating anger, it is a good idea to verbally process the client's experience before undertaking further artmaking.

The indicators do not always represent an impending loss of control. It is not uncommon for survivors to use drawing of self-destructive or violent images as replacement for the actual behavior. The therapist and client need to work together to develop an understanding of the meaning of such indicators in the client's artwork.

The client who is somewhat comfortable with art can be encouraged to initiate drawing for containment and expression when she is angry outside the therapy sessions. Another approach is for the therapist to suggest that the client make a drawing in response to a particular situation that comes up in therapy. When I returned from a short vacation, Sharon, a client, was angry at me but was unable to explain exactly what she was angry about. In response to my suggestion that she make a drawing reflecting her feelings, before the next session she drew a picture with a figure of me towering over a very small figure of her. Above her head was a bubble containing a bomb. Our discussion of the drawing in the therapy session revealed that Sharon had felt "very small" when I left to go on vacation. The feeling of being "very small" was Sharon's way of describing being a child. When I went on vacation, Sharon's feelings of emotional abandonment by her mother were triggered. Exploration through the drawing gave us the means to access Sharon's feelings of anger, to identify the developmental level of her anger (childlike), to clarify transference issues (she was projecting anger at her mother onto me), to understand her disconnection from feelings (the bubble over her head), and to recognize the intensity of feelings (as explosive as a bomb).

Body-Centered Interventions in Working with Anger

Due to the potential for loss of control through physically active expression of anger as described above, the therapist needs to use a certain amount of caution in introducing active body movement with an angry client. Body-centered interventions that are neutral (as opposed to affect-laden) and controlled may contain anger through motor discharge. For example, deep breathing has a calming, regulating effect while providing energy release; tearing paper or tissues confines motor activity to the distal parts while offering tension release. In both examples, energy discharge takes place without actively mobilizing the entire body. Both interventions offer a means of distraction away from anger: Deep breathing is usually accompanied by calming statements; paper tearing often diverts the client from tearing at her fingernails or scratching herself. The paper tearing intervention is no longer containing when the client envisions the paper as the object of her anger; in that situation, the paper is no longer neutral and the intervention is stimulating expression of anger.

ANGER EXPLORATION EXERCISE #1:
LOCATING ANGER IN THE BODY

This exercise can be undertaken when: (1) the client is in the midst of feeling anger; (2) when an event has occurred which would result in most people feeling anger yet the client is not aware of feeling any anger or; (3) when an incident that occurred outside the session elicited anger.

1. Ask the client to identify where in the body the anger is felt. Most people can come up with an answer. If the client is unable to come up with an answer, the therapist can lead the client through a mental body scan, which may yield more results.

2. Have the client describe the sensation caused by anger in that part(s) of the body. Ask the client to use descriptive words and adjectives. The therapist can write down the words and repeat them verbally to the client.

3. If the client has been out of touch with anger, the information gathered thus far may provide sufficient new information for a discussion which focuses on helping the client become more aware of feeling angry in the future. The exercise may be continued to expand the imagery either in the same session or at a later date. Each successive step in this exercise is worthy of a processing discussion and may, in itself, offer sufficient material for one therapy session.

4. Ask the client what color the angry sensation would be if it had a color.

5. Have the client draw the angry sensation (either in the session or as homework).

6. If the client is comfortable with doing body movement exercises in the session, have the client create a body posture or movement that reflects the shape, form, and movement of the drawing. The therapist can verbally describe the client's movements or postures echoing the client's own words. Also, the client can verbalize how she feels during this part of the exercise. If the drawing suggests an explosive or out-of-control movement, have the client use her hands rather than her body to create a movement.

Exploration of anger may occur as the client continues to work on connecting body and mind, identifying body postures and sensations that accompany anger or anger-inducing situations, as described in Chapter 8. The client may need to repeatedly focus on body sensations and the body-felt self in order to begin to be aware of her anger. For several months, Tina's only clue that she was feeling angry was a knot in her stomach. Identification of the knot became her cue to ask herself what she was angry about.

Expression of anger through body movement may be a powerful intervention for the client who has been particularly reticent about expressing emotion. I do not recommend expression of anger through body movement for the client whose anger has been out of control; neutralized motor discharge through sports activities outside of the session is most appropriate in these cases.

In order to effectively express anger through body movement, the client needs to have reached a point in the therapeutic relationship where she can take direction without feeling victimized, resentful, or disempowered. Because angry movement activities have the potential for escalating out of control, the therapist and client should plan the intervention and have agreed that the thera-

---

ANGER EXPLORATION EXERCISE #2:
TRANSFORMING ANGER

The purpose of this exercise is for the client to begin to imagine different ways of responding to anger.

1. Ask the client how she would like to handle anger. Help the client be very descriptive. The client or therapist can write down the descriptive words.

2. Ask the client to make a drawing showing how she would like to handle anger, which may be completed in the session or at home.

3. Process with the client any feelings this exercise elicits as well as the client's thoughts as to what needs to occur in order for her to handle anger in this new way. Sometimes the art will provide clues as to how the client may make a change.

ANGER EXPRESSION EXERCISE #1:
PUNCHING THE PILLOW

This exercise is aimed at the individual who seldom expresses anger or who has not been able to express anger directly. The exercise is tightly structured, beginning with firm limits which may be loosened as the client gains a sense of mastery. When it has been established that the client is able to actively mobilize the body with control, the affective component is then added. The therapist's role in this exercise is to modulate the flow of anger to a safe intensity and to direct the angry movements to a safe object.

1. Make an agreement with the client that you will help her work on her anger if she can agree to work with you. Ask her if she feels she has enough control to follow directions in order to safely express her anger. If the client agrees, proceed with the intervention. If the client cannot agree, postpone working on expression of anger.

2. Explain to the client that the goal is for her to get her anger out in a safe way rather than in an unsafe way. Agree on a verbal statement that will be a signal for the client to stop the intervention. "It's time to stop" or "It's time to calm down" are examples of verbal cues.

3. Have the client take a seated position. Depending on the furniture available in the room, the client may sit in a chair, on a sofa, or on the floor.

4. The therapist should position herself beside the client, one arm's length away from the client, at approximately the same level as the client. For example, if the client is sitting on a sofa, the therapist can be on the sofa or on a chair that is at a similar height. The therapist should be positioned with access to the door in case assistance is needed.

5. An object, such as a big pillow, that can absorb the client's punches should be placed in front of the client.

6. Ask the client to decide how many times she wants to hit the pillow, limiting the number to ten.

7. The therapist demonstrates how to make a fist so that the fingers are curled into the palm. Rings should be removed. If the client has long fingernails, a washcloth, towel, or piece of fabric can be wrapped around the hand and fingers to prevent the nails from gouging into the skin.

Continued

8. The therapist demonstrates how to hit the pillow so that the heel of the hand makes contact with the pillow rather than the knuckles.

9. The client is directed to hit the pillow, counting loudly with each punch until the designated number is reached. If the client is able to maintain control and has not sustained any injury (even minor), then the intervention can be continued. The client and therapist need to check the client's hand to insure that the punching has not caused any cuts or abrasions. At this point, some verbal processing is appropriate.

10. The client is asked to identify the pillow as the person or object at whom she wants to direct her anger. She then is asked to come up with an angry statement she will direct to the person/object while punching.

11. The client is asked once again to choose a number of punches from one to ten. While punching the pillow, she makes the angry statement with each punch. Other angry statements may emerge spontaneously during the punching.

12. To support the client during the punching, the therapist may make encouraging comments, such as: "Say it like you really mean it!" "Let him really hear you." "Show her how angry you are at her." "You're really angry." The therapist should keep track of the number of punches. For instance, after each punch, the therapist can say, "That's one . . . that's two," etc. The client may be reminded when it is time for the last punch as a way to put out a lot of energy while preparing to end the punching. The therapist may make a comment such as, "Give him one last good punch."

13. If the client still needs to discharge anger, has been able to maintain control, and has not in any way hurt her hand, the punching with the verbalization can be repeated.

14. A verbal processing period should follow, addressing how the client felt during the intervention, how the client is feeling after the intervention, and how the client anticipates feeling after the session is over. If appropriate, plans should be made with the client to help her contain herself after the session. The issue of how the client felt showing anger in front of the therapist should be addressed.

pist will stop the intervention if the client begins to show signs of loss of control. As in art work, movement work should be undertaken when the right therapeutic conditions exist. These include a good therapeutic alliance, a safe therapeutic environment, sufficient time in the session to process the experience, and demonstration by the client over time of the ability to use coping skills. A client who is experiencing fantasies of killing herself or others combined with an inability to control impulses is not a good candidate for active anger work; in this situation, anger containment work is most appropriate.

Every client is different and will require individualization. For some clients, for instance, punching a pillow may not be the best approach. Injury can be sustained to the bare hand due to the force of especially powerful punching. Sometimes punching a pillow will quickly decompensate into the client's punching herself; some clients have habitually punched their thighs or other body parts and may have kept this behavior hidden from the therapist or may have been too dissociated during the punching to be fully aware that it was occurring. Harkaway (1991) described a technique whereby the client uses a tennis racket to hit a pillow. Other creative adaptations may be necessary to serve the needs of the individual client. One of my clients remembered that as a child she had wanted to kick her perpetrator during the abuse but had been unable to do so because of the weight of the perpetrator's body on top of her. I used the guidelines described in Anger Expression Exercise 2, replacing the punching with kicking. Not every office has room to accommodate a kicking technique. Pillow punching is perhaps the most portable strategy. For clients who have not had difficulty expressing anger in the past, the therapist can use less structure, allowing the client to hit the pillow repeatedly until the client feels ready to stop. In order for the client to connect angry affect with the source of her anger, punching should be accompanied by verbalizations of anger.

As described above, the potential for loss of control increases when movements are combined with affect and lack of structure, compromising the ability to control connection, modulation, and sequencing. An assessment of the missing or weak control component will allow the therapist to make an intervention that supports the client's needs. For example, Josie began punching her thighs when talking about her stepfather, who was her perpetrator. I handed her a pillow to punch instead of her thighs, changing the *connection* to a different object (the pillow rather than her thighs). However, Josie punched the pillow so hard that she appeared to be bruising her knuckles while getting into a hypnotic punching rhythm. I suggested she lift up her arm higher and punch down on the count of three while she exhaled, adding *modulation* and *sequencing* to her punch.

If Josie had been unable to follow my directions, I would have stopped the intervention, which had thus far safely contained the anger that Josie was expressing. I structured the experience and allowed her to have some discharge without connecting the punching movement with angry affect at her abuser. If I had told her that the pillow was her stepfather, I would have been increasing the affective component, which I would only do once Josie and I had the opportunity to process this experience, since this was Josie's first outward expression of anger in therapy. While pillow punching is a fairly well-known intervention, it can be made more meaningful when the therapist has the knowledge with which to structure a safe, therapeutic experience.

If the following movement indicators appear during an active expression of anger through movement in therapy, the therapist may need to intervene and verbally process with the client what she was feeling at the time to determine if the intervention should continue or be postponed:

1. Perseveration or repetitive movement in a trance state
2. Loss of aim or focus
3. Loss of groundedness
4. Unintelligible verbalizations
5. A sudden change to slashing or scattering movements
6. A change to movements directed at the self

It is important for both the therapist and client to realize that any amount of anger work will provide grist for the therapeutic mill. Any anger work, whether it is interrupted or completed, should be verbally processed after the event, preferably in the same session.

Providing a Safe Environment

Finally, in preparing to do anger work, the therapist needs to provide a safe environment. The client should be situated away from windows to engage in anger work. Decorations such as paperweights that can cause damage if thrown should be removed. The therapist should have easy access to the door in case the client dissociates and tries to attack the therapist. The risk of a dangerous loss of control is probably quite small if the therapist and client have laid the groundwork to do anger work. However, the wise therapist prepares the environment for both the client's and the therapist's protection rather than take the risk.

I learned to heed this advice through my own heart-stopping experience. In the midst of doing anger work with a client who had no history of aggressive behavior and had seldom expressed any anger at all in the past, I suddenly realized that she was punching a pillow very close to the large picture window in my office. As her punching movements built in intensity, she became dissociative and I had a panicky moment when I thought her fist might smash into the window. I simply had not expected her anger to present any potential for danger and, in fact, there would have been no cause for concern if I had more judiciously situated the client in regard to the safety of the environment.

Case Vignette: Joanne

Joanne was unable to feel anger at all. She felt this "anger stuff" was a mystery. After nine months in therapy, she verbally reconstructed a memory of a rape at the age of five—still with no affect. However, soon after she finished describing the rape, she began to shake, explaining that she was feeling anger. I gave Joanne a pillow to punch. First I asked her to punch the pillow as hard as she could three times. Then I asked her who she wanted to punch. She replied that she wanted to punch her uncle, who had assaulted her. I then asked her what she wanted to say to her uncle when she punched him. Her immediate reply was, "I hate you." I suggested she punch the pillow five times while stating, "I hate you." After three punches, she said that she felt nauseous, her heart was racing, and she was beginning to see black all around her. At that point, I stopped the anger work, had her

---

ANGER EXPRESSION EXERCISE #2:
DRAWING ANGER

The client is to make a drawing or collage expressing her anger, which may be completed in a therapy session or at home. This allows the client to externalize feelings of anger, get some physical discharge, and gain a sense of mastery over the emotion. Some clients will draw concrete images depicting angry events, while others will draw abstract images depicting angry feelings. Clients may find this exercise helpful outside of therapy sessions in order to divert angry acting out or to gain a greater sense of mastery over anger. The client may want to use large paper to allow freer expression of affect.

In processing the art, the following questions may be helpful:

1. How were you feeling when you made the picture?

2. What led up to your decision to make the picture (if done outside of therapy)?

3. What is the picture saying about anger?

4. Is there anything new that you learned about anger by making the picture?

5. How did you feel when you finished the picture?

6. Tell me about each of the images/objects/people in the picture.

7. What feeling does the picture convey?

8. Does the picture remind you of any past experience or event?

---

change her position to a different chair in my office, and we processed the experience. Joanne decided that she was not ready to undertake any more anger work because she was fearful of losing control.

Six months later, Joanne reconstructed the rape in more detail. She once again expressed no affect during the reconstruction. The next week she came to her session describing feeling angry at the world. She was ready to do more anger work and we made an agreement that if she felt nauseous she would immediately let me

---

ANGER EXPRESSION EXERCISE #3:
ANGRY TEARING

The purpose of this exercise is to provide an opportunity to direct anger at a representation of a particular individual, such as a perpetrator or a nonprotective parent.

1. The client draws a picture of the person at whom the anger is to be directed or writes the person's name on a piece of paper (paper should be at least 8½ x 11 inches).

2. The client tears the paper into small pieces. Each tearing movement is an opportunity to discharge anger. The client may be encouraged to verbally express anger during the tearing.

3. When the paper is completely torn up, the client is asked to find some way to end the anger work. I have worked with clients who have come up with the following endings: (1) throwing the scraps in a wastebasket; (2) taking the scraps home to burn them; (3) stamping on the scraps and then throwing them in the wastebasket; (4) asking the therapist to throw the scraps away somewhere outside of the office.

Variations on this approach have been suggested by Westerlund (1992): tearing a large, heavy sheet of paper with the word "incest" or "perpetrator" written on it; destroying a photograph of the perpetrator; and defacing a drawing of a representation of the abuse such as a bed or of the perpetrator such as a piece of clothing.

NOTE: Tearing paper (or tissues) without projecting the source of anger onto the paper serves as a good containment technique, especially when the client has the urge to hurt herself and is in need of safe motor discharge.

---

know and we would stop the intervention. She was having difficulty visualizing her uncle in her mind in order to focus her anger on him. I had her draw a picture of her uncle. I then asked her what she wanted to say to him. With some hesitation she was able to tell him, "I hate you." At that point, she told me that she was beginning to feel shaky. I asked her how old she was feeling

and she responded five years old. I asked her how she could remember that she was an adult while she talked to her uncle. She
identified that holding on to her wedding ring helped her feel like
an adult. While she held onto her wedding ring, I asked her once
again what she would like to say to her uncle. This time she
immediately replied, in a firm, clear voice, "You'll never hurt me
again." I then asked her if there was anything she would like to
do to the picture. She took a black marker and drew an "X" across
her uncle's face. Then she tore the picture up in small pieces,
repeating "You'll never hurt me again" several times. She tore each
piece into smaller and smaller pieces, until a pile of paper slivers
was on my desk in front of her. Joanne stated that using her hands
helped her feel like an adult because as a child her hands had been
tied while her uncle raped her. I then asked her what she would
like to do with the paper scraps. She recalled that there was a
dumpster near my office and decided to throw them there when
she left the office. Although she was still feeling angry, she was
able to develop a series of anger management strategies, including
fast-walking every day and deep breathing, that she successfully
used outside of the therapy sessions.

The pillow in the first session and the paper in the second
session provided safe objects with which the client could connect
her anger. Because Joanne was ready to actively work on anger
expression, I suggested that the pillow represent her abuser; if we
had been working on containment, I would have allowed the pillow to remain a neutral object without suggesting that it represent
her abuser. In the first session, I created structure, modulation,
and sequencing by suggesting that Joanne punch the pillow five
times. In the second session, she did not need any support in
modulating her strength because she tore up the paper with even
movements. By asking Joanne what she wanted to do with the
scraps of paper, I was sequencing the experience in order to arrive
at an ending for the anger work.

13
DEVELOPING A SENSE OF SELF

THE RESOLUTION OF THE SEXUAL abuse trauma releases the survivor from her identity as a victim. Having accepted that she was not at fault for the abuse while acknowledging that she now has choices, she is free to focus her energy on developing herself. Perhaps for the first time, she may begin to consider that she has a future, one that is aimed at pursuing her own personal goals rather than struggling with the aftereffects of her victimization. Judith Herman (1992) eloquently describes the survivor's task at this stage:

> Her task now is to become the person she wants to be. In the process she draws upon those aspects of herself that she most values from the time before the trauma, from the experience of the trauma itself, and from the period of recovery. Integrating all of these elements, she creates a new self, both ideally and in actuality. (p. 202)

Rediscovering Playfulness and Spontaneity

The process of creating a new self often involves rediscovering parts of the self which may have been forgotten or denied. Many survivors who became parentified at a young age may reclaim the child-self, rediscovering spontaneity and playfulness. Long-forgotten interests, hobbies, and passions may resurface. For the survivor who does not have immediate access to the child-self, activities and objects reminiscent of childhood may trigger a connection. Looking at toys, books, and photographs or observing a child or children may be a good catalyst to remembering the child-self. If the survivor is looking to become more spontaneous or playful, I may suggest finger-painting or smearing-type drawing with chalk pastels, which may be undertaken as part of a therapy session or as homework. Because of the potential for regression when using an art medium that uses smearing or the fingers, the therapist needs to carefully weigh the client's potential for decompensation during such an activity.

Fifteen years ago, when I was in graduate school, Dianne Dulicai introduced me to a movement exercise which provides an opportunity to redo childhood through movement. The exercise helped several of my survivor clients reclaim the more playful aspects of childhood that they had missed. I recommend that the exercise be completed as a homework assignment. The survivor experiences the development of body skills leading up to adulthood. For example, beginning with the simple tasks of infancy, the client may begin by holding up her head, grasping objects, crawling, walking, skipping, leading up to adolescence or adulthood. Because clients may have blanks in their childhood or be unfamiliar with a "normal" childhood, the therapist and client may first review the developmental tasks, making a chronological list of movement skills. The emphasis for the client in undertaking the exercise is to experience body movement as positive, joyful, and free.

Reinventing Self and Others

The survivor may contemplate how she would have been different if aspects of herself that were stifled because of the abuse had been allowed to flourish. She may feel an enormous sense of grief over what has been lost. She may also use her imagination to create experiences or aspects of herself that would otherwise not exist. In an effort to feel what it would have been like to have been loved by her father, Joan made a collage entitled, "Daddy Reinvented," through which she imagined having a loving father.

RECLAIMING CHILDHOOD THROUGH
BODY MOVEMENT

1. The client will experience the development of movement skills beginning in infancy and ending in adulthood. This exercise should be done as homework or as a group therapy activity. The emphasis is on doing the activities as if for the first time rather than on reliving past experiences.

2. The client may need help familiarizing herself with a chronology of movement skills, such as:

   • lifting the head
   • grasping objects
   • sitting up
   • crawling
   • standing up
   • walking
   • spinning
   • playing stop and go
   • jumping up and down
   • skipping
   • dancing
   • playing sports

3. Any activities that elicit feelings or memories present good material for processing.

NOTE: In deciding whether to undertake this exercise, the therapist and client should be aware that the activities of infancy may invite regression.

The exploration of "Daddy Reinvented" brought Joan closer to acknowledging the hurt her father caused her and helped her accept that she deserved love and caring as a child. Creating what might have been through art simultaneously taps into feelings of loss and entitlement. However, recreating the past cannot erase or undo the damage. Joan's work with "Daddy Reinvented" contributed to her self-esteem through her recognition that she deserved a loving father.

Picking an Apple from an Apple Tree

A drawing task that I have found to be extremely rich and powerful in investigating obstacles to self-actualization is to have the client draw a picture of herself picking an apple from an apple tree (Furth, 1988). A task of unknown origin (Emmanuel F. Hammer, personal communication, May, 1990), the apple tree metaphor is such an obvious parallel to achieving goals that clients find it unusually easy to interpret. When Monica, age 19, wanted to leave therapy after two months in order to go back to college out of state, I asked her to draw a picture of herself picking an apple from an apple apple tree (Figure 21). The most important feature of the drawing was that she was unable to reach the apple despite the fact that she was standing on a platform. She interpreted the platform to represent the supports in her life and concluded that her supports were not sufficient to help her successfully return

Figure 21   *Picking an apple from an apple tree*

to school. Unfortunately, this insight did not prevent Monica from prematurely returning to school, where she was asked to withdraw after failing the semester. Before she left, I asked her to draw the picture again, this time showing herself reaching the apple, including anything that she might need in order to pick the apple. She was unable to come up with any ideas that would assist her in getting closer to her goal, further attesting to her lack of readiness to return to school.

Clients are usually truly surprised when they discover that they have drawn themselves unable to reach the apple, a reflection of feelings of helplessness. Sometimes the person in the drawing has a ladder or some kind of support to reach the apple that actually looks weak or precarious, possibly indicating a precarious support system. A drawing may have apples scattered on the ground with the client drawn high up on a ladder, perhaps reflecting an individual who makes things more complicated than they actually are,

---

PICKING AN APPLE FROM AN APPLE TREE

Instructions to client:
"Draw a picture of yourself picking an apple from an apple tree."
General discussion question:
"If this drawing were to represent how you go about getting what you want in life, what would it say about you?"
Some of the aspects of the drawing to consider are:
- The tree—How full is it? How alive is it?
- The apples—How many are there?
- The person—Is there anything unusual?
            How does she get the apple?
            Is she actually getting the apple?
            If not, does it look like she will?
            If not, what's getting in her way?
            How does she feel?
For the client who did not get the apple in the drawing:
Consider the appropriateness of having the client draw the picture with whatever supports may be needed so that she will get the apple. Discuss the drawing, identifying supports in the client's life that may facilitate her reaching her goals.

misses the obvious, or enjoys risk-taking for its own sake. The client is ultimately the only person who can confirm the correct meaning of the picture.

Sometimes the client's understanding of her sense of helplessness and inadequacy through the drawing is extremely painful. In those situations, the therapist may suggest that the client redraw the picture with whatever helps or resources she might need in order to attain the apple. Some clients may need help in visualizing themselves successfully picking the apple.

The therapeutic benefit of the drawing is that the client can assess her current ability to self-actualize, can ascertain obstacles to self-actualization, and can create new solutions to problems.

Reclaiming Sexuality

Frequently, at this point in the therapy clients are ready to actively work on sexuality. The client may want to conquer specific difficulties surrounding sexual relations with a partner or she may simply want to become more comfortable with herself as a sexual being. Dolan (1991) advises:

> In talking frankly about sensuality and sexuality, the therapist must model an obvious sense of healthy comfort, so that the client can openly discuss any difficulties she is experiencing and identify possible solutions. Empowering a formerly sexually abused client to reclaim her sexuality may be a delicate step for the therapist. It is imperative that the client not feel intruded upon, lest the invasive aspects of the original trauma be symbolically reenacted. (p. 165)

Together, the therapist and client problem-solve how the survivor may become more comfortable with sex or sexuality. At times, the survivor may need to work on assertiveness in order to be able to tell her partner that she needs to abstain from sex or needs to make certain changes in her sexual habits.

Nancy found her only view of sexuality was linked to shame and self-hate. She initiated the project of making two collages: one was of women from a lingerie catalogue, which reminded her of healthy adult sexuality; the other was of famous women whom she saw as "healthy sexual women," role models she had never known. She also collected songs to which she danced at home; her favorite was Aretha Franklin singing, "Natural Woman." To dance in a session with me not only would have been too embarrassing for her but also would have potentially violated the boundaries of our relationship. We were able to discuss her dancing; she was especially delighted with being able to freely shake her hips and wiggle her pelvis, movements which she had previously found too threatening. I referred her to an Afro-Caribbean dance class, which gave her a safe, structured opportunity to continue to enjoy the freeing movements.

When the client is ready to explore sexuality, a body scan may give her information about areas of her body that are blocked, rigid, or in conflict over experiencing healthy sexuality. Outside of the therapy, the client may attempt dance, exercise, and other body-centered activities that will allow the body to be freer, more open, and more relaxed. For the client who is comfortable moving in a therapy session, she can try a sitting or walking posture/movement that expresses her body as open and free.

As the client feels more confident, she may be ready to try the safe touch activities described in Chapter 8, in which the client strokes her arms, face, and hands. The survivor may want to expand the stroking movement in order to begin exploring sensuality and sexuality, noticing the difference between sensual and sexual sensations, and between sensual and sexual touching. This is an activity that the client should do at home, so that she can freely experience any sexual sensations that may result. I was pleased to discover that Elaine Westerlund (1992), who researched women survivors' sexuality, suggests similar self-touch and body awareness exercises in her book, *Women's Sexuality after Childhood Incest*.

The Future Self

The survivor may have missed not only the joy of childhood, but also the chance to explore and consolidate her identity in adolescence or young adulthood. Annie, age 39, described her experience: "It's like I missed out on being a teenager and I don't know who I am and I don't know who I want to be and I don't know how to talk, how to be social with people."

BEING THE FUTURE SELF

1. Have the client clearly imagine the future self. For the client who has no spontaneous images of herself in the future, the therapist may use a guided imagery exercise such as that described by Napier (1990, p. 125). Have the client focus on the qualities of the future self.

2. Have the client visualize the way the future self is in her body.

   - How does the future self sit?
   - What does her body feel like?
   - What kind of posture does she have?
   - How does she walk?

   Now have the client experience the future self in her own body, asking the same questions. Ask the client to verbally describe the experiences as she sits, moves, walks. Repeat her verbalizations as she sits, moves, and walks as the future self.

3. Suggest that the client continue to experience the future self when she leaves your office, sitting, standing, and moving as the future self.

4. The client may make a drawing or a collage that embodies the qualities of the future self.

The survivor, who has found her voice through the telling of her story of abuse, is now ready to use her voice to be heard in social and work situations. Annie confronted her supervisor at work, saying that she was no longer going to allow herself to be disrespected. She also began to socialize more. Perhaps one of her most visible signs of recovery was her decision to dress in brightly colored clothing; feeling a new sense of safety, she was ready to be visible in the world. In an effort to take better care of her body, she quit smoking and started an exercise program.

Annie had been working as a waitress for years and claimed that she had never had any vocational goals. However, as women in her therapy group began to pursue long-forgotten career goals first formed in childhood, Annie's envy motivated her to develop her own goals. My initial suggestion to her was to fantasize outside of therapy and imagine seeing herself doing some kind of work she would enjoy. Annie's self-doubts were triggered by this suggestion. She expressed her fears that she was stupid and that she would make a fool of herself pursuing a goal that was beyond her abilities. At this point in the therapy, we simultaneously explored Annie's self-doubts while developing an image of a "future self" (Napier, 1990), one that represented new aspirations for herself in the future. As Napier suggests, the future self embodies qualities rather than content.

The view of Annie's future self that initially emerged was ot a new sense of determination that she was "going to make something of myself." A drawing of herself picking an apple from an apple tree depicted Annie being lifted by the women in her therapy group. She was clutching an apple with both hands. Her interpretation of the drawing was that she needed the continued support of the group in order to pursue a career goal. In describing the manner in which she was picking the apple, she stated, "I'm holding onto that apple for dear life and I am not going to let go." She saw her two-handed approach as symbolic of her need to work very hard and give her all to pursuing a career goal. She was also excited by the determination the drawing depicted.

Annie eventually decided to enroll in college part time to work toward a bachelor's degree in social work. At the age of 39, she would be finding herself in the unaccustomed role of student. Her newfound determination was evident in a collage showing herself as a college student and social worker. She entitled the collage, "I can do it," reflecting her new identity as a strong, determined women.

I also encouraged her to develop a sense of her future self in her body, first focusing on internal sensations. Then I directed her to walk around my office in the style of her future self. Annie discovered that her future self's posture was very much like her posture when she was feeling strong and in charge of her life. This insight helped her feel more confident in her ability to achieve her career goal, as she recognized that her new sense of self included aspects of her already existing self.

The increased sense of confidence typical of survivors in this phase of therapy may be reflected in their body attitude. While

Figure 22   *"How I will feel when I like (love) my body"*

the future self will display the confident body attitude in a more extreme way, at this point the survivor may be able to recognize a new sense of confidence in the increased erectness of her posture and the greater feeling of certainty in her movements. The journey from victim to survivor bolsters the survivor's use of stronger movements and her increasingly vertical postures.

Tanya made a drawing which she called "How I will feel when I like (love) my body" (Figure 22) which shows a vertical posture with arms reaching upward toward the sky. An interesting feature of the drawing is the alligator under the base of the platform. Reptilian creatures frequently represent sexuality or sexual abuse. In the drawing Tanya appears to be triumphing over the alligator, although she was quite unconscious of its presence and meaning.

The development of a sense of self may lead the survivor to feel a new sense of creativity. Drawing may be undertaken for the mere joy of self-expression. The change in the survivor's identity may be evident in changing artistic styles and propensities. For instance, Gina began to use bright colors after two years of drawing in pencil. She also started to experiment with watercolors and signed up for a painting class.

As the survivor continues to rework the abuse trauma throughout the rest of her life, she will be armed with a wide array of coping skills, an internalized sense of safety, a support system, and a clearly defined sense of self—all gained through therapy. A review of her therapy, illustrated by her drawings, provides a visual record of her journey and her progress. An exploration of the changes in her relationship with her body during the course of therapy establishes a kinesthetic knowledge of her progress. The reexamination of her work further consolidates the sense of self and affirms that the survivor has succeeded in transforming the silence of childhood into the language of adulthood. In discovering her voice, she begins to transcend her identity as a survivor of childhood sexual abuse to become uniquely and fully herself.

REFERENCES

American Psychiatric Association (1987). *Diagnostic and statistical manual of mental disorders, 3rd edition, revised.* Washington, DC: American Psychiatric Association.

American Psychiatric Association (1993). *DSM-IV draft criteria.* Washington, DC: American Psychiatric Association.

Bass, E., & Davis, L. (1988). *The courage to heal: A guide for women survivors of child sexual abuse.* New York: Harper & Row.

Baum, E. Z. (1991). Movement therapy with multiple personality disorder patients. *Dissociation, 4,* 99–104.

Baum, E. Z. (1993). Dance/movement group therapy with multiple personality disorder patients. In E. S. Kluft (Ed.), *Expressive and functional therapies in the treatment of multiple personality disorder.* Springfield, IL: Charles C Thomas.

Belenky, M. F., Clinchy, B. M., Goldberger, N. R., & Tarule, J. M. (1986). *Women's ways of knowing: The development of self, voice, and mind.* New York: Basic Books.

Bernstein, D. A., & Borkovec, T. D. (1973). *Progressive relaxation training: A manual for the helping professions.* Champaign, IL: Research Press.

Bernstein, E., & Putnam, F. W. (1986). Development, reliability, and validity of a dissociation scale. *Journal of Nervous and Mental Disease, 174,* 727–735.

Biggins, T. S. R. (1989). *An outline of a preliminary investigation of the nonverbal characteristics of sexually abused, primary school-aged girls.* Unpublished master's thesis. Hahnemann University: Philadelphia, PA.

Birren, F. (1961). *Color psychology and color therapy.* New York: University Books.

Blake-White, J., & Kline, C. M. (1985). Treating the dissociative process in adult victims of childhood incest. *Social Casework: The Journal of Contemporary Social Work, 66,* 394–402.

Blume, E. S. (1990). *Secret survivors.* New York: Ballantine.

Boor, M. (1982). The multiple personality epidemic. Additional cases and references regarding diagnosis, etiology, dynamics and treatment. *Journal of Nervous and Mental Disease, 170,* 302–304.

Braun, B. G. (1988a). The BASK model of dissociation. Part 1. *Dissociation*, 1(1), 4–23.

Braun, B. G. (1988b). The BASK model of dissociation. Part 2: Clinical applications. *Dissociation*, 1(2), 16–23.

Breuer, J., & Freud, S. (1893–95). *Studies on hysteria*. In J. Stratchey (Ed. & Trans.), *The standard edition of the complete psychological works of Sigmund Freud*. Vol. II. New York: Norton.

Briere, J. (1989). *Therapy for adults molested as children: Beyond survival*. New York: Springer.

Briere, J., & Conte, J. (1993). Self-reported amnesia for abuse in adults molested as children. *Journal of Traumatic Stress*, 6(1), 21–33.

Briere, J., & Courtois, C. A. (1992, June 28). *The return of the repressed: Memory retrieval*. Workshop presented at the Fifth Eastern Regional Conference on Abuse and Multiple Personality, Alexandria, VA.

Browne, A., & Finkelhor, D. (1986). Impact of child sexual abuse: A review of the literature. *Psychological Bulletin*, 99, 66–77.

Buck, J. N. (1948). The H-T-P technique: A qualitative and quantitative scoring manual. *Journal of Clinical Psychology*, 4, 317–396.

Burns, R. C., & Kaufman, S. H. (1970). *Kinetic family drawings (K-F-D): An introduction to understanding children through kinetic drawing*. New York: Brunner/Mazel.

Calof, D. L. (1992, June 28). *Self-injurious behavior: Treatment strategies*. Workshop presented at Fifth Eastern Regional Conference on Abuse and Multiple Personality, Alexandria, VA.

Cappacchione, L. (1988). *The power of your other hand*. North Hollywood, CA: New Castle Publishing.

Chace, M. (1975). The role of the arts in therapy. In H. Chaiklin (Ed.), *Marion Chace: Her papers*. Columbia, MD: American Dance Therapy Association. Reprinted from *The Northwestern University Reviewing Stand* (Nov. 11, 1951), 17, 3–9.

Chutis, L. (1990). Flashbacks. In E. Sue Blume (Ed.), *Secret survivors: Uncovering incest and its aftereffects in women*. New York: Wiley.

Cohen, B. M. (1992a). Art in therapy by non-specialists. *Treating abuse today*, 2(4), 13–14.

Cohen, B. M. (1992b, June 27). *The expressive therapies continuum: Structure and process*. Workshop presented at the Fourth Annual Eastern Regional Conference on Abuse and Multiple Personality, Alexandria, VA.

Cohen, B. M., & Cox, C. T. (1989). Breaking the code: Identification of multiplicity through art productions. *Dissociation*, 2, 132–137.

Cohen, B. M., & Hammer, J. S., & Singer, S. (1988). The Diagnostic Drawing Series: A systematic approach to art therapy evaluation and research. *Arts in Psychotherapy*, 15, 11–21.

Cohen, F. W., & Phelps, R. E. (1985). Incest markers in children's artwork. *The Arts in Psychotherapy*, 12, 265–283.

Combs, G., & Freedman, J. (1990). *Symbol, story, and ceremony: Using metaphor in individual and family therapy*. New York: Norton.

Comstock, C. M. (1993). Believe it or not: The challenge to the therapist of patient memory. *Treating Abuse Today*, 2(6) 23–26.

Coons, P. M., & Milstein, V. (1984). Rape and post traumatic stress in multiple personality: Characteristics, etiology and treatment. *Journal of Clinical Psychiatry*, 55, 839–845.

REFERENCES

Courtois, C. A. (1988). *Healing the incest wound: Adult survivors in therapy.* New York: Norton.

Courtois, C. A. (1991). Theory, sequencing, and strategy in treating adult survivors. In J. Briere (Ed.), *Treating victims of child sexual abuse. New Directions for Mental Health Services, 51.* San Francisco: Jossey-Bass.

Courtois, C. A. (1992). The memory retrieval process in incest survivor therapy. *Journal of Child Sexual Abuse, 1*(1), 15–32.

Davis, M. (1966). An effort-shape movement analysis of a family therapy session. Unpublished paper available from Dance Notation Bureau.

Davis, M. (1977). *Methods of perceiving small group behavior.* New York: Dance Notation Publications.

Davis, M. (1981). Movement characteristics of hospitalized psychiatric patients. *American Journal of Dance Therapy, 4*(1), 52–71.

Davis, M. (1983). An introduction to the Davis nonverbal analysis system (DaNCAS). *American Journal of Dance Therapy, 6,* 49–73.

Davis, M., & Hadiks, D. (1987). The Davis nonverbal states scales for psychotherapy research: Reliability of LMA-based coding. *Movement Studies, 2,* 29–34.

DeArment, M. (1993). *Movement characteristics of an individual with multiple personality disorder.* Unpublished master's thesis. Hahnemann University, Philadelphia, PA.

Dell, C. (1977). *A primer for movement description: Using effort shape and supplementary concepts.* New York: Dance Notation Bureau.

Deutch, F. (1947). An analysis of postural behavior. *Psychoanalytic Quarterly, 16,* 195–213.

Dolan, Y. M. (1991). *Resolving sexual abuse: Solution-focused therapy and Ericksonian hypnosis for adult survivors.* New York: Norton.

Dosamantes-Alperson, E. (1981). The interaction between movement and imagery in experiential movement psychotherapy. *Psychotherapy: Theory, Research, and Practice, 18*(2), 266–270.

Dulicai, D. (1976). Dance therapy and its research. *Bulletin of the International Conference on Nonverbal Communication, 1*(3), 16–18.

Fast, J. (1970). *Body language.* New York: Evans.

Flannery, R. B. (1987). From victim to survivor: A stress management approach in the treatment of learned helplessness. In B. A. van der Kolk (Ed.), *Psychological trauma.* Washington, DC: American Psychiatric Press, Inc.

Freud, S. (1905). Three essays on sexuality. In J. Strachey (Ed. & Trans.), *The standard edition of the complete psychological works of Sigmund Freud.* Vol. VII. New York: Norton.

Freud, S. (1915–16). Introductory lectures on psychoanalysis. In J. Stratchey (Ed. & Trans.), *Standard edition.* Vol. XV. New York: Norton.

Frye, B., & Gannon, L. (1990). The use, misuse and abuse of art with dissociative/multiple personality disorder patients. *Occupational Therapy Forum, 5*(25), 3–5.

Fuhrman, N. L. (1993). Art and multiple personality disorder: A developmental approach to treatment. In E. S. Kluft (Ed.), *Expressive and functional therapies in the treatment of multiple personality disorder.* Springfield, IL: Charles C Thomas.

Furth, G. M. (1988). *The secret world of drawings: Healing through art.* Boston: Sigo.

Galbraith, N. (1978). A foster child's expression of ambivalence. *American Journal of Art Therapy, 17,* 39–49.

Gelinas, D. (1983). The persisting negative effects of incest. *Psychiatry, 46,* 312–332.

Gendlin, E. T. (1978). *Focusing.* New York: Bantam Books.

Gil, E. (1988). *Treatment of adult survivors of childhood abuse.* Walnut Creek, CA: Launch Press.

Gil, E. (1991, November 1). *Treatment of sexual abuse survivors.* Training seminar presented at The Horsham Clinic, Ambler, PA.

Gil, E. (1993, February 26). *Special issues in the treatment of childhood abuse.* Seminar presented in Philadelphia, PA.

Goodill, S. W. (1987). Dance/movement therapy with abused children. *The Arts in Psychotherapy, 14,* 59–68.

Greenberg, S. A. (1982). *Sexually abused girls: An examination of their D-A-P's and K-F-D's.* Unpublished master's thesis. Hahnemann University, Philadelphia, PA.

Greenberg, M. S., & van der Kolk, B. A. (1987). Retrieval and integration of traumatic memories with the "painting cure." In B. A. van der Kolk (Ed.), *Psychological trauma.* Washington, DC: American Psychiatric Press, Inc.

Grinder, J., & Bandler, R. (1981). *Trance-formations.* Moab, UT: Real People Press.

Hammer, E. F. (1954). Guide for qualitative research with the H-T-P. *Journal of General Psychology, 51,* 41–60.

Hammer, E. F. (1978). *The clinical application of projective drawings.* Springfield, IL: Charles C Thomas.

Harkaway, J. (1991, May 10). *Women who hurt themselves.* Seminar presented at the Philadelphia Child Guidance Clinic.

Herman, J. L. (1992). *Trauma and recovery.* New York: Basic Books.

Herman, J., & Schatzow, E. (1987). Recovery and verification of childhood sexual trauma. *Psychoanalytic Psychology, 4,* 1–14.

Hoffman, W. (1991). The body remembers? *Voices in Action Conference* (91VA10A). Minneapolis: Resurrection Tapes.

Holroyd, J. C., & Brodsky, A. M. (1977). Psychologists' attitudes and practices regarding erotic and nonerotic physical contact with patients. *American Psychologist, 32,* 843–849.

Holroyd, J. C., & Brodsky, A. M. (1980). Does touching patients lead to sexual intercourse? *Professional Psychology, 11*(5), 807–811.

Horowitz, M. J. (1978). *Image formation and cognition. 2nd edition.* New York: Appleton-Century-Crofts.

Howard, R. (1990). Art therapy as an isomorphic intervention in the treatment of a client with post-traumatic stress disorder. *The American Journal of Art Therapy, 28,* 79–86.

Howard, M., & Jakab, I. (1969). Case studies of molested children and their art productions. *Psychiatry and Art, 2,* 72–79.

Hyde, N. D., & Watson, C. (1990). Voices from the silence: The use of imagery with incest survivors. In T. A. Laidlaw, C. Malmo, & Associates (Eds.), *Healing voices: Feminist approaches to therapy with women.* San Francisco: Jossey-Bass.

Jack, D. C. (1991). *Silencing the self: Women and depression.* Cambridge, MA: Harvard University Press.

Jacobson, M. L. (1985). Manifestations of abuse in the artwork of an inpatient diagnosed with multiple personality disorder. In B. G. Braun (Ed.), *Dissocia-*

tive disorders: Proceedings of the Second International Conference on Multiple Personality and Dissociative Disorders. Chicago: Rush Presbyterian-St. Luke's Medical Center.

Jacobson, M. L. (1986). *Managing anger in the MPD patient: Therapeutic approaches through art*. (ID-303-86). Alexandria, VA: Audio Transcripts.

Jacobson, M. L. (1990). *At risk indices of suicide in the artwork of the patient with MPD*. (VIIID-59-90). Alexandria, VA: Audio Transcripts.

Jacobson, M. L. (1993). Group art therapy and multiple personality disorder. In E. S. Kluft (Ed.), *Expressive and functional therapies in the treatment of multiple personality disorder*. Springfield, IL: Charles C Thomas.

Jacobson, M. L. & Mills, A. (1992). *A survey of art therapy in the identification and treatment of MPD*. (34-742-92). Alexandria, VA: Audio Transcripts.

Janet, P. (1889). *L'automatisme psychologique*. Paris: Bailliere.

Janoff-Bulman, R. (1992). *Shattered assumptions: Towards a new psychology of trauma*. New York: Free Press.

Jehu, D., Klassen, C., & Gazan, M. (1985-1986). Cognitive restructuring of distorted beliefs associated with childhood sexual abuse. *Journal of Social Work and Human Sexuality, 4*, 1–35.

Jung, C. G. (1952). *The collected works*. London: Routledge & Kegan Paul.

Kagan, S. L., & Lusebrink, V. B. (1978). The expressive therapies continuum. *The Arts in Psychotherapy, 5*(4), 171–179.

Kaplan, B. J. (1991). Graphic indicators of sexual abuse in drawings of sexually abused, severely emotionally abused, disturbed children and nondisturbed children. *Dissertation Abstracts International, 52*(2), 1065B (University Microfilms No. ADG91-21476).

Kaufman, B., & Wohl, A. (1992). *Casualties of childhood: A developmental perspective on sexual abuse using projective drawings*. New York: Brunner/Mazel.

Kelly, S. (1984). The use of group therapy with sexually abused children. *Journal of Psychosocial Nursing, 22*(12), 12–18.

Kendon, A. (1979). Movement coordination in social interaction: Some examples described. In S. Weitz (Ed.), *Nonverbal communication: Readings with commentary*. New York: Oxford University Press.

Kestenberg, J. (1975). *Parents and children*. New York: Aronson.

Kluft, E. S., Poteat, J., & Kluft, R. P. (1986). Movement observations in multiple personality disorder: A preliminary report. *American Journal of Dance Therapy, 9*, 31–46.

Kluft, R. P. (1990). Incest and subsequent revictimization: The case of therapist-patient sexual exploitation, with a description of the sitting duck syndrome. In R. P. Kluft. (Ed.), *Incest-related syndromes of adult psychopathology*. Washington, DC: American Psychiatric Press, Inc.

Kluft, R. P. (1992, October). *Speak, memory: Challenges in the interpretation of autobiographical recollections of childhood abuse*. Paper presented at the Institute of Pennsylvania Hospital, Philadelphia, PA.

Kramer, E. (1971). *Art as therapy with children*. New York: Schocken.

Kramer, S., & Akhtar, S. (Eds.)(1992). *When the body speaks: Psychological meanings in kinetic cues*. Northvale, NJ: Jason Aronson.

Kreuger, D. W. (1990). Developmental and psychodynamic perspectives on body-image change. In T. F. Cash & T. Pruzinsky (Eds.), *Body images: Development, deviance, and change*. New York: Guilford.

Krieger, M. J. (1991). Developing an internalized protector. In W. N. Friedrich (Ed.), *Casebook of sexual abuse treatment*. New York: Norton.

Kris, E. (1952). *Psychoanalytic explorations in art*. New York: International Universities Press.

Krystal, H. (1979). Alexithymia and psychotherapy. *American Journal of Psychoanalysis, 33*, 17–31.

Lerner, M. J. (1980). *The belief in a just world*. New York: Plenum.

Levick, M. F. (1967). The goals of the art therapist as compared to those of the art teacher. *Journal of Albert Einstein Medical Center, 15*, 157–170.

Levick, M. F. (1983). *They could not talk and so they drew: Children's styles of coping and thinking*. Springfield, IL: Charles C Thomas.

Levy, F. J. (1988). *Dance movement therapy: A healing art*. Reston, VA: American Alliance for Health, Physical Education, Recreation, and Dance.

Lindemann, E. (1944). Symptomatology and management of acute grief. *American Journal of Psychiatry, 101*, 141–148.

Lister, E. D. (1982). Forced silence: A neglected dimension of trauma. *American Journal of Psychiatry, 139*(7), 872–876.

Loftus, E. F. (1993). The reality of repressed memories. *American Psychologist, 48*(5), 518–537.

Lowen, A. (1958). *Physical dynamics of character structure*. New York: Grune & Stratton.

Lubin, B., Larsen, R. M., Reed, M., & Matarazzo, J. D. (1984). Patterns of psychological test usage in the United States: 1935–1982. *American Psychologist, 39*(4), 451–454.

Lusebrink, V. B. (1990). *Imagery and visual expression in therapy*. New York: Plenum.

Machover, K. (1980). *Personality projection in the drawing of the human figure*. Springfield, IL: Charles C Thomas.

Malchiodi, C. A. (1990). *Breaking the silence: Art therapy with children from violent homes*. New York: Brunner/Mazel.

Maltz, W. (1991). *The sexual healing journey*. New York: HarperCollins.

Maltz, W., & Hoffman, B. (1987). *Incest and sexuality*. Lexington, MA: Lexington Books.

Malmo, C., & Laidlaw, T. A. (1990). Afterword: Empowering women through the healing process. In T. A. Laidlaw, C. Malmo, & Associates (Eds.), *Healing voices: Feminist approaches to therapy with women*. San Francisco: Jossey-Bass.

McCoubrey, C. (1990). Rhythms of recovery: A movement perspective on dissociation. In B. G. Braun & E. B. Carlson (Eds.), *Dissociative disorders: Proceedings of the Seventh International Conference on Multiple Personality and Dissociative States*. Chicago: Rush Presbyterian-St. Luke's Medical Center.

McCann, I. L. , & Pearlman, L. A. (1990). *Psychological trauma and the adult survivor: Theory, therapy, and transformation*. New York: Brunner/Mazel.

Meiselman, K. (1990). *Resolving the trauma of incest: Reintegration therapy with survivors*. San Francisco: Jossey-Bass.

Milakovich, J. (1992). *Touching in psychotherapy: Therapists who touch and those who do not*. Doctoral dissertation, The Fielding Institute, Santa Barbara, CA.

Miller, A. (1981). *The drama of the gifted child: The search for the true self*. New York: Basic Books.

REFERENCES

Mills, A., & Cohen, B. M. (1993). Facilitating the identification of multiple personality disorder through art: The diagnostic drawing series. In E. S. Kluft (Ed.), *Expressive and functional therapies in the treatment of multiple personality disorder*. Springfield, IL: Charles C Thomas.

Napier, N. J. (1990). *Recreating your self: Help for adult children of dysfunctional families*. New York: Norton.

Napier, N. J. (1993). *Getting through the day: Strategies for adults hurt as children*. New York: Norton.

Naumburg, M. (1966). *Dynamically oriented art therapy: Its principles and practice*. New York: Grune & Stratton.

North, M. (1972). *Personality assessment through movement*. Boston: Plays.

Novaco, R. W. (1975). *Anger control: The development and evaluation of an experimental treatment*. Lexington, MA: Lexington Books.

Ogden, D. (1977). *Psychodiagnostics and personality assessment: A handbook. 2nd edition*. Los Angeles: Western Psychological Services.

Oster, G. D., & Gould, P. (1987). *Using drawings in assessment and therapy: A guide for mental health professionals*. New York: Brunner/Mazel.

Perls, F., Hefferline, R. F., & Goodman, P. (1977). *Gestalt therapy*. New York: Bantam.

Putnam, F. W. (1989). *Diagnosis and treatment of multiple personality disorder*. New York: Guilford.

Putnam, F. W., Guroff, J. J., Silberman, E. K., Barban, L., & Post, R. M. (1986). The clinical phenomenology of multiple personality disorder: A review of 100 recent cases. *Journal of Clinical Psychiatry, 47*, 285–293.

Reich, W. (1949). *Character analysis*. New York: Farrar, Straus & Giroux.

Rorschach, H. (1942). *Psychodiagnostics*. Bern: Verlag Hans Huber.

Rubin, J. A. (1983). Media potential. Its use and misuse in therapy. In A. DiMaria, E. S. Kramer, & E. A. Roth (Eds.), *Art therapy: Still growing. Proceedings of the 13th Annual Conference of the American Art Therapy Association*, 114–115.

Ryder, D. (1992). *Breaking the circle of satanic ritual abuse: Recognizing and recovering from the hidden trauma*. Minneapolis: CompCare.

Schmais, C. (1974). Dance therapy in perspective. In K. C. Mason (Ed.), *Dance therapy, Focus on Dance VII*, Washington, DC: AAHPER.

Schultz, R., Braun, B. G., & Kluft, R. P. (1985). Creativity and the imaginary companion phenomenon: Prevalence and phenomenology in MPD. In B. G. Braun (Ed.), *Dissociative Disorders: Proceedings of the Second International Conference on Multiple Personality and Dissociative States*. Chicago: Rush Presbyterian-St. Luke's Medical Center.

Sgroi, S. (1989). *Vulnerable populations: Sexual abuse treatment for children, adult survivors, offenders, and persons with mental retardation*, Vol. 2. Lexington, MA: Lexington Books.

Sidun, N. M., & Rosenthal, R. H. (1987). Graphic indicators of sexual abuse in Draw-A-Person Tests of psychiatrically hospitalized adolescents. *The Arts in Psychotherapy, 14*, 25–33.

Singer, J. L. (1974). *Imagery and daydream methods in psychotherapy and behavior modification*. New York: Academic Press.

Spaletto, C. C. (1993). Individual art therapy with the hospitalized multiple personality disorder patient. In E. S. Kluft (Ed.), *Expressive and functional therapies in the treatment of multiple personality disorder*. Springfield, IL: Charles C Thomas.

Spring, D. (1986a). Symbolic language of sexually abused, chemically dependent women. *American Journal of Art Therapy, 24,* 13–21.

Spring, D. (1986b). *The visual language of multiplicity.* (ID-303-86). Alexandria, VA: Audio Transcripts.

Spring, D. (1988). Sexual abuse and post-traumatic stress reflected in artistic symbolic language. Ann Arbor, MI: Dissertation Abstracts International.

Spring, D. (1993). Artistic symbolic language and the treatment of multiple personality disorder. In E. S. Kluft (Ed.), *Expressive and functional therapies in the treatment of multiple personality disorder.* Springfield, IL: Charles C Thomas.

Steele, K., & Colrain, J. (1990). Abreactive work with sexual abuse survivors: Concepts and techniques. In M. Hunter (Ed.), *The sexually abused male: Application of treatment strategies, Vol. 2.* Lexington, MA: D. C. Heath.

Stember, C. J. (1980). Art therapy: A new use in the diagnosis and treatment of sexually abused children. In B. McComb Jones, L. L. Jenstrom, & K. Mac-Farlane (Eds.), *Sexual abuse in children: Selected readings* (pp. 59–63). Washington, DC: U. S. Government Publications.

Summit, R. C. (1983). The child abuse accommodation syndrome. *Child Abuse and Neglect, 7,* 177–193.

Sutherland, S. (1991). Movement therapy. In *Expressive therapies in the identification and treatment of dissociative disorders.* 32ABCDE. Alexandria, VA: Audio Transcripts.

Turkus, J. (1990). *Survival kit for therapists working with MPD.* (23-669-90). Alexandria, VA: Audio Transcripts.

Wadeson, H. (1980). *Art psychotherapy.* New York: Wiley.

Weltman, M. (1986). Movement therapy with children who have been sexually abused. *American Journal of Dance Therapy, 9,* 47–66.

Westerlund, E. (1992). *Women's sexuality after childhood incest.* New York: Norton.

Wilbur, C. B. (1984). Multiple personality and child abuse. *Psychiatric Clinics of North America, 7,* 3–7.

INDEX

accommodation syndrome, 2
adult body posture, 22, 95, 96, 141
affect:
  art as expression of, 99–102
  assessment in memory work, 139–140
  in BASK model, 143–144
  blockage in head-body split, 109–111
  as body-felt sense, case vignettes of, 112–116
  containment of flooding in, 92–95
  controlled expression in, 96–97
  fear of loss of control in expression of, 103–104
  inability to verbalize, 111–112
  nonverbal expression of, 104
  in PTSD, 7
  somatic locations of, 105–107, 111
  strategies for building awareness of, 104–108
  see also anger; anger work; flooding symptoms
Akhtar, S., 5, 18
alexithymia, 8–9
American Psychiatric Association, 7, 8, 127
amnesia, 143
  in PTSD, 7–8
anger:
  extratherapeutic release of tension from, 157–158
  learned suppression of, 155–156
  in middle phase work, 15
  somatic manifestation of, 23, 105, 156–158
  see also anger work

anger work:
  art-centered interventions in, 162–165, 173
  body/movement-centered interventions in, 165–171
  case vignette, 172–175
  client control in physical expression activities, 158, 162, 170
  continuum of interventions, 158–160
  exploratory questions, 161
  goal of, 160
  in groups, 160–161
  indications for, 161–162, 170
  interrupting physical expression in, 171
  intolerance of affect in, 162
  locating anger in the body, 166
  pillow punching exercise, 168–169, 170–171, 175
  safe environment for, 172
  therapeutic alliance and, 161, 162, 167–170
  transforming exercise, 167
anxiety:
  drawing as controlled discharge of, 99–101
  manifestations of, 76–78
  as PTSD symptom, 77
art-centered interventions:
  in anger work, 162–165, 173
  apple tree metaphor in, 179–181, 184
  art production in therapy session, 28–29
  assessment through, 26, 36, 45–65
  choice of media in, 30
  client-initiated, 26–28